The Blue Guide
Written Communication for Leaders in Law Enforcement

Elizabeth Brockman

Preliminary Edition

PEARSON CUSTOM PUBLISHING
75 Arlington Street, Suite 300, Boston, MA 02116
A Pearson Education Company

CONTENTS

PREFACE

Welcome to the first edition of *The Blue Guide: Written Communication for Leaders in Law Enforcement*. A unique writing handbook for cadets and police officers, it was developed from a long standing and well respected workshop sponsored by the Police Executive Leadership College (PELC). In this workshop, participants learn a universal truth about written communication, a truth embraced by successful professionals working in countless companies, institutions, and departments across many fields, disciplines, and industries. Written communication is an important professional activity. As such, writing in the workplace can never be passed off as merely bureaucratic paperwork or even correct grammar, as law enforcement personnel have traditionally believed. Instead, written communication is linked to leadership, and so good writing—regardless of a writer's rank or experience level—has the power to do the following:

- Build a writer's self-image.
- Reinforce professional relationships.
- Enhance public relations.
- Promote policies and programs.
- Increase *esprit de corps*.

With these truths as cornerstones, *The Blue Guide* is designed to foster excellent written communication skills in, most obviously, the modern police officer. However, *The Blue Guide* also has the power to enhance the written communication of future professionals in other disciplines because the author is not a police officer; she's an English professor. As the "About the Author" explains (see p. xi), the author has extensive professional experience working with police officers; however, her credentials more generally cover writing, the teaching of writing, and business/professional communication. As a result, police-related topics, such as Miranda Rights or line-up procedures, may "come up" in the myriad writing samples selected for the book, but these concepts are not introduced as learning objectives because *The Blue Guide* is strictly a writing handbook, one designed for police officers but with tremendous versatility and flexibility.

The Blue Guide is divided into three overlapping sections with self-explanatory chapter titles. Part I (The Power of the Pen: Becoming a Law Enforcement Leader) has four chapters: Understanding the Power of the Pen, Putting Grammar in its Place, Writing Concise Sentences, and Monitoring Paragraph Length. Part II (Effective Police Reports: Leading by Example) has two chapters: Defining the Police Report as Genre and Celebrating Three Police Officers. Part III (Administrative Documents: Leading with the Written Word) has three chapters: Leading with Purpose, Incorporating Indented Lists, and Articulating Reader Benefits. *The Blue Guide* ends with four useful appendices. Appendix A showcases a basic format for memos and letters, Appendix B outlines ten strategies for good visual impact, Appendix C focuses on resume writing, and Appendix D provides an overview of the PELC program, which is the inspiration for *The Blue Guide*.

Throughout *The Blue Guide*, readers can count on the following special features:

- **Accessible Chapters.** Each chapter is organized to maximize visual appeal, reader interest, and concept accessibility:

  Chapter Opening. Each chapter begins with three featured sections: An inspirational quote about the power of the written word, "Leadership Objectives," and "Assess Yourself." A brief introduction follows.

  Major Content. Major content naturally varies from chapter to chapter; however, each chapter includes clear content descriptions followed by specific examples and illustrations taken directly from actual police documents.

  Closing. Each chapter ends with the following sections: "Chapter Review," Discussion Questions," and "Test Yourself."

- **Authentic Writing Samples.** As previously indicated, *The Blue Guide* is filled with writing sample after writing sample—including sentences, paragraphs, and whole documents—taken directly from current police files. This important feature is a common thread throughout each major section and individual chapter, lending credibility and accessibility to the entire handbook.

- **"Looking Back" Boxes.** *The Blue Guide* includes countless "Looking Back" boxes. These boxes prompt readers to remember a key concept or issue from a previous chapter and consider it in light of a new writing sample or concept. This important feature reinforces the overlapping nature of the chapters and, more importantly, encourages deeper learning and promotes stronger writing skills.

ACKNOWLEDGMENTS

I must begin these acknowledgements by remembering my long-time mentor and dear friend, Dr. Kitty O. Locker, who was an English professor at the Ohio State University where I earned my graduate degrees. Kitty introduced me to business and professional communication as a discipline, supervised me in my early professional communication classes, and then recruited me to lead my first PELC workshop. It changed my life. After directing my dissertation, she strongly encouraged me to pursue a teaching career at the university level where I would have the time and resources to write, and I followed that advice. Though Kitty never read a single draft of *The Blue Guide*, her contribution is immense. I miss her.

I also extend special thanks to the hundreds of PELC workshop participants who proposed in the first place that I publish a writing handbook with police officers in mind. Over the years, their encouragement for the book has been consistently augmented by rave workshop reviews, and I am humbled and honored by their collective support and appreciation of my work. In addition, I salute my PELC colleagues: Dr. Ted Darrow, Dr. Ted Oakley, and Monica Poling. Ted Darrow and Ted Oakley provided morale support at the beginning of this book project, and Monica helped locate the contact information for the dozens of police leaders whose written work is showcased in the book. In the final days, Ted Oakley assisted in creating Appendix E, which is an overview of the PELC program.

Next, I offer appreciation and affection to my Central Michigan departmental colleagues: Marcy Taylor, Melinda Kreth, and Mary Ann Crawford; Susan Stan, Susan Griffith, and Henry Fulton. In one way or another, each of these individuals provided support and inspiration.

In addition, I thank the editorial staff at Allyn and Bacon. In particular, David Repetto has been an incredibly kindhearted, candid, and patient editor as I worked through the drafting of *The Blue Guide*. I will always be grateful that he was named acquisitions editor of the Criminal Justice Department at Allyn and Bacon when I submitted my book manuscript.

Last and most importantly of all, I thank Tim Brockman and our three children: Ann Marie, Katie, and Andy. Awake, awake to love and work!

ABOUT THE AUTHOR

Dr. Elizabeth Brockman has worked as a PELC workshop leader since 1993. Since then, she has taught hundreds of Ohio police leaders in her practical, interactive, and entertaining workshops on written communication. Her respect for law enforcement leaders, love of subject matter, and enthusiasm for teaching are three factors contributing to the success of her workshops. In response to participants' requests, Dr. Brockman has written *The Blue Guide: Written Communication for Leaders in Law Enforcement.*

Dr. Brockman is currently a tenured English professor at Central Michigan University, where she teaches composition and composition methods courses at the undergraduate and graduate levels. Additionally, she supervises student teachers with English majors and graduate assistants teaching ENG 101. Her BA (1983) is from the English Department at Michigan State University, and both her MA (1988) and PhD (1995) are from the English Department the Ohio State University. She has published articles in *English Journal, Language Arts Journal of Michigan, The Writing Instructor, Women's Issues in Literacy* and *Life Assembly, Journal of Business Communication,* and *Business Communication Quarterly.* In addition, she is associate editor for *Pedagogy: Critical Approaches to Teaching Literature, Language, Composition, and Culture,* an award winning national journal published by Duke University Press.

Dr. Brockman lives in Michigan with her husband, Tim Brockman, and their three children: Ann Marie, Katie, and Andy.

PART ONE

THE POWER OF THE PEN: BECOMING A LAW ENFORCEMENT LEADER

Men and women pursue law enforcement careers for a variety of reasons: a desire for a better world, a sense of justice and order, the belief that one person can make a difference. Nobody, however, seems to join the field because they "love to write." It's a fact, one that comes as no surprise because police officers aren't technically writers in the same way that journalists, publishers, or PR specialists are. These folks write for a living. In fact, it's all they do. When we imagine them at work or see pictures of them on TV or in magazines, we see people with pen/paper, at computers, or in some other writing-related activity or setting.

Not so with police officers.

Nevertheless, police officers (and all white-collar professionals, for that matter) should remember that publishers, journalists, and PR specialists are not the only wordsmiths in the professional world. Sales executives, bankers, accountants, and managers, for example, all write on the job, most often under severe time constraints. They may not define themselves as writers—in other words, writing may not be their primary on-the-job responsibility—but writing is an essential component of their professional identities and work lives. Moreover, the better these professionals write—the more effectively and efficiently they know how to convey a message to a target audience—the more successful they will become in their chosen careers and the more likely it is they will become leaders in their companies and fields.

As evidence, consider the wise words of a professional named Derek van der Merwe. Van der Merwe is not a sales executive, banker, accountant, or manager, but he is a wordsmith and a true leader in his organization and field. Van der Merwe is a university athletics director and a national expert on compliance for Division I Athletics. At a recent workshop comparing (a) careers in writing and (b) careers that require writing, van der Merwe explained that "after high school or college and in the real world, writing is the key to success. Whatever your professional interests and goals may be, you are more likely to achieve them if you are a good writer." Van der Merwe went on to explain that pure knowledge of Division I compliance rules, standards, and mandates was essential, *but not sufficient*, to guarantee professional success and leadership status in university athletics. He needed to combine that pure compliance knowledge with effective and efficient written communication skills to perform a variety of professional duties: to write reports supporting or disciplining student-athletes and coaches, to inform relevant parties about compliance topics and to persuade them of their importance, and to foster professional relationships among student-athletes, parents, and coaches, as well as athletics administrators, college professors, and university officials at both his home institution and across the sports conference. It was this combination of compliance knowledge *and written communication skills* that distinguished van der Merwe from other compliance directors and promoted his success and leadership.

The same is true for police officers. To be successful, they must obviously understand state and federal laws, departmental policies and procedures, and community norms and values. This knowledge is essential, and no one can deny it. However, pure knowledge is not enough to be successful in law enforcement. To be successful, an officer must be able to convey ideas effectively and efficiently in written words—often under severe time constraints—and, perhaps most importantly, *see the value in doing so*. In short, a law enforcement police officer must believe in the Power of the Pen.

There is, however, no Power of the Pen "conversion moment." It doesn't happen automatically upon high school, college, or police academy graduation. It doesn't take place when a police badge is bestowed or at the time of a first arrest or conviction; and for some, it never happens at all. Some officers—and they may be good people who do their jobs with honor and pride—believe that writing is nothing more than bureaucratic BS, a simple matter of paper shuffling and brown nosing. Others mistakenly believe that writing is nothing more than a matter of correct grammar and usage. However, *The Blue Guide* is designed to debunk those myths and help you understand and acquire the Power of the Pen. It's important to remember, though, that no single book—not even an innovative book designed especially for police officers—can by osmosis provide any cadet, officer, or ranked officer with the Power of the Pen. It takes time, practice, and the right attitude to reinforce that the written word really does make a difference. Part I of *The Blue Guide*—The Power of the Pen: Becoming a Law Enforcement Leader—will help you on your journey.

Part I is divided into four chapters. Chapter One explains the Power of the Pen. More specifically, it explains the dramatic way the written word can bring about positive or negative change, including (1) building or breaking a writer's self-image, (2) enhancing or eradicating PR, (3) promoting or impeding policies and procedures, and (4) increasing or annihilating *esprit de corps*. In addition, the chapter showcases three hallmarks of effective writers. Chapter Two puts grammar in its place by targeting the top ten grammar mistakes most likely to be found in police documents, Chapter Three highlights five strategies for writing concise sentences, and Chapter Four teaches strategies for monitoring paragraph length.

CHAPTER ONE

UNDERSTANDING THE POWER OF THE PEN

I write to inform, recognize, motivate, inspire, and celebrate individual police officers and the Cincinnati Police Department.

Captain Gene A. Hamann, Night Chief
Cincinnati Police Department
Cincinnati, Ohio

Leadership Objectives

- To recognize the importance of writing in the field of law enforcement.
- To understand the Power of the Pen; the written word can (a) build or break a writer's self-image, (b) enhance or eradicate public relations, (c) promote or impede policies/programs, and (d) increase or annihilate esprit de corps.
- To identify three hallmarks of effective writers. They tend to consider "the big picture" for any written document, to recognize that writing is a process, and to understand that writing is a developmental skill.

Assess Yourself

Ask yourself the following questions:

- Do you define yourself as a writer?
- Are good writers born that way, or do they learn to be good writers?
- Do you have confidence in yourself as a writer? Why?
- What types of documents, topics, and occasions prompt you to write?
- What is your writing process? Do you tend to write documents in one sitting? Describe your typical behavior when you are in the act of writing? Does your writing process depend on the time you have available to write or the complexity/familiarity of the document to be written?
- Do you believe that an interest in writing process implies there is always "time to spare" when it comes to writing?
- How much writing do you believe police officers do on the job?

To begin understanding the Power of the Pen, read the following five scenarios, paying special attention to the gap between leadership intentions, pure knowledge, and writing skills:

Scenario #1: A Commendation

A police chief learns that a new officer did an especially good job investigating a domestic violence case. His interviewing skill made the difference. He not only interviewed people carefully, but he also compared interviewees' comments and, as a result, discovered key discrepancies even seasoned officers had missed. To commend the new officer, the police chief calls him into his office and warmly congratulates him on a job well done. Moreover, he explains that he has heard of countless other exemplary investigations on the part of the officer. It's clear to the chief that the new officer is a "cut above the rest" and is a credit to both his police academy and department. He tells the young man that he hopes he will keep up the good work.

A year later, the new officer is nominated for a distinguished service award. When his personnel file is pulled, the award committee sees solid performance evaluations but nothing more—no commendation letters or "atta boys"—and so the award goes to another officer.

Scenario #2: A Promotion Request

A police officer of five years learns of a position currently open for a sergeant in another department. The officer has earned the respect of her shift members and superiors, and she feels she is ready for a promotion, so she gathers the appropriate application materials, including solid recommendations, excellent performance evaluations, an updated resume, and an application letter. Two weeks before the deadline, she drives to the other department so she can hand deliver the entire packet to the chief, who is impressed by the officer's professional demeanor, confidence, and promptness.

However, the officer doesn't realize that her resume and application letter are filled with grammar mistakes, wordy sentences, and poor organization. Despite persuasive recommendations and excellent evaluations, the officer is not offered the position because of her poor writing skills.

Scenario #3: A Proposal for a K9 Unit

A captain in a rural department believes a K9 unit would enhance local investigations. He has completed the research and knows that the start-up and maintenance expenses for a K9 unit are affordable, and he actually boasts firsthand K9 experience in another jurisdiction. Instead of writing a formal proposal, the captain shares his ideas with both the chief and mayor in informal conversations—every chance he gets.

Before long, the chief and mayor grow weary of the captain's "broken record," so the K9 idea is never taken seriously. As a result, the police department and the entire community don't benefit from a K9 unit.

Scenario #4: A Police Report

A police officer is dispatched to the scene of a minor traffic accident. In the middle of interviewing drivers, though, he is called away on a more serious dispatch. He suggests the two drivers exchange information and then hurries off, without time to take notes. At the end of his shift, the officer completes his paperwork but forgets to write a report for the accident. Days later, one driver calls to say that his insurance agency requires a police report for even minor repairs, but because the officer forgot to write a report, there is no record of the accident on file. After searching, the dispatch record is discovered, and the police officer is asked to write/submit the report.

The officer easily pulls together the information for a report; however, the driver is disturbed by the apparent disorganization on the officer's part, which also reflects poorly upon the entire police department.

Scenario #5: A Directive

A lieutenant is frustrated by the unprofessional dress of third-shift officers. Their uniforms are often wrinkled, their shoes are not shined, and they often don't wear regulation haircuts. Even worse, the lieutenant has specifically asked officers to clean up their acts, but they simply aren't obeying. Their apparent lack of respect seems to be calling into question the lieutenant's authority, and he is frankly angered by it. The last straw is when a new officer comes to roll call wearing an earring. "What's the big deal?" the officer defensively asks, "I'll take it out before hitting the road." After losing his temper in front of the entire platoon, the lieutenant goes straight to his computer where he fires off an angry email, berating the officer in question but letting the entire shift know he will no longer tolerate unprofessional dress and/or insubordination.

By writing the email, the lieutenant documents an important procedure, which is good; however, his angry tone is unprofessional, and it does not promote positive change, good PR, or honorable self-image.

In each scenario, the writer has leadership intentions and law enforcement knowledge. In Scenario #1, the chief wants to commend the new officer. In Scenario #2, the officer deserves a promotion. In Scenario #3, the captain wants to improve local investigations. In Scenario #4, the officer knows how to write an effective police report. In Scenario #5, the lieutenant's directive is valid. Nevertheless, none of the officers achieves his/her leadership purpose, and each time the reason is the same: ineffective writing. None of the officers (ranked or unranked) in the five scenarios seems to understand the Power of the Pen.

THE POWER OF THE PEN

What is the Power of the Pen? In the field of law enforcement, it means that the written word—regardless of whether it relates to a police report written by a new officer or a policy statement written by the police chief—has the power to bring about positive or negative change. More specifically, the written word has the power to do the following: build or break a writer's self-image, enhance or eradicate pubic relations, promote or impede policies and procedures, and increase or annihilate *esprit de corps*. Understanding the Power of the Pen helps police officers write more effectively and efficiently.

Build or Break a Writer's Self-Image

A well written report, letter, or press release (or any other police document) makes a police officer look good. Readers may never actually meet the officer, but if his/her written communication has clear purpose, good visual impact, proper format, and excellent diction, it reflects positively on the police officer and department. In contrast, when written communications are sloppily completed, the officer's integrity and competence are compromised both then and in the future, and it reflects poorly on the entire police department too.

Looking Back

Think back to Scenario #2: A Commendation. How did the poorly written resume and application letter hurt the officer's self-image? Do you think she might have been promoted if her written materials had been more carefully prepared? Do you think she is likely to be hired by the same department in the future?

Looking Back

Think back to Scenario #5: A Directive. Did the lieutenant have a right to be angry? Even so, how did the angry email hurt the lieutenant's self-image?

Enhance or Eradicate Public Relations

Written documents have the power to promote good PR. It's a win-win situation, for example, when police officers write documents promptly and professionally to personnel in, for example, the DA's Office, the public schools, a community organization, or local businesses. Regardless of format or purpose, the simple act of writing promotes goodwill and demonstrates competence.

Looking Back

Think back to Scenario #4: A Police Report. The officer eventually wrote the accident report, but he submitted it late. Why did his tardiness anger the citizen? How did it hurt his professional image and eradicate PR for his department?

Looking Back

Think back to Scenario #2: A Promotion Request. Does the officer's sloppy resume and application letter diminish PR with the nearby police department?

Promote or Impede Policies and Procedures

Policies and procedures are always documented in writing, so writing quality will naturally influence success or failure. Policies/programs must be written in language that is clear, accessible, logical, and fair-minded. Moreover, the content or substance of the policies/programs must be consistent with department bylaws or union contracts, and it should include measurable objectives. If any of these important elements is missing, readers are less likely to understand policies and procedures, and so they will be less able or willing to follow them.

Looking Back

Think back to Scenario #3: A Proposal for a K9 Unit. The K9 unit would have benefited the rural district. Why do you think the captain didn't take the time to write a proposal? How might the proposal have changed the outcome?

Looking Back

Think back to Scenario #5: A Directive. Do you believe that the lieutenant's email promoted or impeded departmental policy regarding dress code? Why?

Increase or Annihilate *Esprit de Corps*

Writing has the power to promote teamwork and build morale, and both concepts are monumentally important in the field of law enforcement. Though individual effort and personal initiative are crucial, police officers must ultimately work cooperatively and collaboratively as a unit or platoon to "get the job done," whatever that job may be. That's why *esprit de corps*, which is a French phrase meaning "team spirit," is so important. One of the best ways to build *esprit de corps* is through the written word. A simple and heartfelt "thank you" after roll call or during a hallway encounter, for example, is a good start; however, this word of thanks takes on far greater significance when it is put in writing. The very act of writing formalizes the message, making it public and granting it permanence.

Looking Back

Think back to Scenario #1: A Commendation. The new officer surely appreciated his chief's kind words in the meeting; however, would he have appreciated even more the same words documented in writing and placed in his personnel file?

Looking Back

Think back to Scenario #3: A Proposal for a K9 Unit. The captain was surely discouraged by the chief's and mayor's lack of response. Would a written response have bolstered the captain's morale? Does it depend on the type of written response? Why?

THREE HALLMARKS OF EFFECTIVE WRITERS

Effective writers are not born that way. They have learned attitudes and behaviors that render them effective. This section showcases three major values and/or behaviors: understanding "The Big Picture," recognizing that writing is a process, and believing that writing is a developmental skill.

The Big Picture

Effective writers know that any written document—a report, a vacation request, a commendation, an equipment request, as four examples—is more than a series of words, sentences, and paragraphs linked together to form a page or a series of pages. Instead, effective writers know that any written document is a complex, professional, and much needed response to a specific set of special circumstances; and in the field of law enforcement, circumstances vary widely from day to day and even hour to hour. To clarify, consider the following range of circumstances a police department might face on any given day:

Table 1.1: Six Circumstances

- A child has been abducted from her backyard. She was last seen being driven away against her will in a green sedan at 10:00 AM.
- The DARE officer at a local middle school has reported late to work four times in the last six weeks.
- The city has purchased new laptops for all sworn police officers, and a training course will take place in two weeks. Attendance is mandatory.
- A parade route has changed at the last minute.
- A foreign diplomat will arrive, along with secret service agents, next Tuesday.
- Two teenagers were caught driving under the influence during their school lunch hour.

These six circumstances would naturally trigger or prompt any police officer into action; one of the actions, however, would be to write one, two, three or even several different documents in a relatively short amount of time. The effective police officer sees the Big Picture for each set of circumstances and reacts quickly by recognizing the inherent similarities and differences among them and *how they will influence a writer's choices*. To begin recognizing the Big Picture concept, first imagine what types of documents each of the six circumstances might prompt. For example, if a parade route is suddenly changed, what kinds of documents would need to be quickly written and why? Similarly, what kinds of documents might a police officer write upon learning that a DARE officer had been irresponsible or that a foreign diplomat were arriving, and what would the time-frames be? What kind of writing would be required ASAP in response to a child abduction or an MIP? Try to list at least two or three different kinds of documents for each set of circumstances.

Looking Back

As you create the list of documents for each set of circumstances, keep in mind the Power of the Pen. Any document you propose should do one or more of the following:

- Build self-image.
- Enhance Public relationships.
- Promote policies and procedures.
- Increase *esprit de corps*.

   In other words, how will the documents you list help to bring about positive change, regardless of the circumstances, in a police department and community?

After listing these documents, consider the Big Picture: What is the primary purpose for each document? In other words, why is the writer writing? What message needs to be conveyed? Consider the following possibilities: to inform, to persuade, to alert, to direct, to publicize, to update, to report, to document, to prioritize, to apologize, to commend (to name just a few of the nuanced reasons that police officers are called to write). Second, who is the audience for each document? More specifically, is the audience an internal or external person? Would s/he be most accurately described as a subordinate, an equal, or a superior in relation to the writer, and how would the audience's relationship to the writer influence choices? Also, is the audience comprised of one, two, three, or more people or even groups of people? In other words, is the audience a single audience or a multiple audience? Third, what form or genre should the document be? Does the form/genre influence the writer's page length, overall organization, level of formality, and word choice? Last (and for the sake of argument), consider how purpose, audience, and/or form would either alter slightly or radically change if the police department were located in (a) a thriving metropolis, (b) a suburban community, (c) a rural area, or (d) a college campus?

Be ready to justify your perspective in a classroom or workshop setting, where there is ample time and opportunity to share multiple views and perspectives. In the process, though, don't forget that effective police officers consider these questions automatically, perhaps even instinctively, on the job because they are constantly working under severe time constraints.

Looking Back

Return to Table 1.1: Six Circumstances. Name three additional circumstances that police departments face each day, and then ask the Big Picture questions:

- What kind of documents might the circumstances prompt?
- What is the purpose of each document?
- Who is the audience?
- What is the form/genre of the document?

   Last, consider how the answers might change if the police department/city were located in an urban, suburban, rural, or college community area.

Writing as a Process

Only inexperienced and/or ineffective writers tackle all writing tasks in the same uniform way, typically sitting down cold and knocking out virtually every kind of document from start to finish without looking back, except for a quick spell or grammar check as the final step. To clarify, consider the following hypothetical situations:

- A graduating cadet writes his first resume for a job opening in a nearby police department. The day before the application deadline, he pulls up a generic resume form from the Internet and "plugs in" his own credentials. After spending an hour on this important document, he does a quick spell and grammar check and figures the document is "good to go," but it really isn't. The generic format doesn't showcase the cadet's special qualifications, and the cadet hasn't given himself time to remember all relevant awards and experiences that might be persuasive to potential employers. As a result, his resume isn't as effective or professional as it could be (see Appendix D for information about effective resume writing).
- A new police officer sets aside thirty minutes at the end of her shift to write five reports. Her notes are unclear and it's hard to remember all details from several hours ago, but she has no choice at the moment but to plow through each report from start to finish, with just a quick confirmation regarding the accuracy of names/contact information and crime classification. When her shift supervisor reads the reports, he finds substantive mistakes regarding criminal investigations, as well as surface errors in grammar/usage, and so he asks the new officer to resubmit ASAP.
- A police chief is thoroughly dismayed when he hears that the recently elected mayor plans to reduce healthcare for city employees. In response, he fires off an angry email, questioning the mayor's lack of foresight and disloyalty. The mayor is surprised and offended by the chief's angry note, and their professional relationship begins with a rocky start.

What is wrong with each of these writing situations? What do they all have in common? First of all, none of the writers has taken into consideration The Big Picture, as it is defined in the previous section. In other words, they have not taken into serious consideration purpose, audience, or (in some cases) format. Second, all of the writers are drafting *unfamiliar documents* in one sitting. This is huge professional mistake! The cadet has never written a resume before, and it's not clear that he has researched the police department in question, and the new police officer is inexperienced at writing police reports in her new position; and though the police chief has obviously written countless emails, his document has unfamiliar elements: a new audience (the recently elected mayor) and an unfamiliar topic (the new healthcare plan). Besides all this, the chief is writing in anger.

Experienced writers know better. They full understand the need for efficiency when it comes to writing, but they also understand that writing is a process, one that varies from writer to writer and from document to document. To clarify this concept, consider for just a moment the processes of three tasks totally different from writing: hoisting a sail, installing a hard drive, or knitting an afghan (all labor-intensive tasks far less complex than police writing). How long does each activity take and how much energy will be exerted? What will the process be? These questions are ultimately impossible to answer because it depends on a number of variables, most of them human. Here, for example are three of those variables:

- The Person's Experience. Is the person a novice? If yes, does the person have the aptitude or previous experience to learn the activity in question or is she/he "all thumbs," as the saying goes? Is there a mentor to guide the novice or are "how to" guides available? If the person has experience at the activity in question, has he/she learned the activity thoroughly and practiced often? Does the person truly know how to complete the activity in question?
- The Person's Motivation. Does the person see value in the activity? Does she/he have a positive or negative attitude? Is she/he willing to put forth the effort to learn and/or complete the activity?
- The Environment. Is there proper weather and/or lighting? Are the necessary tools accessible and of good or low quality? If something breaks or becomes otherwise dysfunctional, are resources available to correct the situation?

All of these variables would make a difference in the process of hoisting a sail, installing a hard drive, or knitting an afghan, and though writing differs from these activities in significant ways, we can apply the same basic principles. How long a document takes to write and how much energy a writer exerts depends entirely on the writer and his/her expertise and motivation. To clarify, consider the following:

- A veteran police officer spends literally minutes writing an excellent report regarding an incident of domestic violence. Over the years, he has written dozens of domestic violence reports, including at least six recent reports regarding the parties involved in his current report, so the process is routine for him. No wonder he can write so quickly. However, when the same officer is asked to participate for the first time in a grant writing initiative, he spends thirty minutes simply looking over the application guidelines without even picking up a pencil—except to take some notes.
- A lieutenant spends more time than usual on a one-page reprimand regarding an officer's misconduct. He has written reprimands previously with far more efficiency, but this particular document is complicated because the officer in question has a spouse who is both a city employee and a good friend of city attorney. These relationships shouldn't make any difference in theory, but the lieutenant wisely recognizes that—human nature being it is—his document will be carefully scrutinized by a wider audience than usual, and he wants to represent himself and his department to the very best of his ability. Just to be sure, he asks his chief to serve as a second reader.
- A police officer reflects that her shift supervisor typically approves her reports, passing them on immediately to chief's designee for final approval before submission to the DA's Office. The same shift supervisor routinely asked the officer for revision work regarding crime classification and probably cause during the first few months after training. In addition, the officer notices that she writes reports far more quickly than she used to write them.

What do these three writing situations have in common? What can we learn from them? In each case, the police officer in question wisely and intuitively varies his/her writing process depending on the situation, and the key variable is not necessarily time available; instead, it's *document familiarity and, by extension, complexity.* The more familiar and less complex the writing task is, the more efficiently the writer writers. The veteran officer has written dozens of domestic violence reports, so he can compose them effortlessly and within minutes; that's not the case, though, for grant writing. Likewise, the lieutenant's writing process naturally lengthens when he must write about an officer whose conduct is complicated by strong ties to the city offices, especially the attorney's office. Does this mean that the lieutenant can spend all day writing? Do his schedule and job responsibilities allow him to close his office door and ignore the rest of the department? Of course not! It simply means that reprimands, in general, have become routine with years of practice writing them, whereas THIS reprimand is more complex and so it requires a little more finessing. Finally, the relatively new officer has noticed that her writing process is more efficient (she needs to spend less time writing and then revising at her supervisor's request) as she gains practice in writing reports. It makes perfect sense.

So how does a police offer balance writing process and time constraints inherent in the field of law enforcement? First of all, they should understand that an interest in or a discussion about of writing processes does not imply unlimited time exits when it comes to writing. On the contrary, police officers have some of the most hectic schedules in the professional world, so there is never "time to spare." Even if there were, though, no self-respecting police officer would close his/her office door and spend the entire day writing; it just isn't part of police culture. On the other hand, even over-tasked police officers wisely acknowledge that poorly written documents are likely to waste time on "the other end" of the writing process—that is, after distribution takes place, when external and/or internal audiences are confused, puzzled, or even angry over an unclear message. The point here is simple: Police officers must always strive for efficiency when it comes to writing; however, unfamiliar and/or complex documents often require more time to write, but this time is wisely spent because it helps to eliminate the need for damage control later.

The question, of course, how does a police officer balance writing process and time constraints? What strategies are worth a police officer's valuable and limited time? What strategies may actually save time in the long run? Perhaps most importantly of all, which strategies will, with practice, become second nature?

To answer these questions, remember that most experienced writers across disciplines divide the writing process into four stages: planning, drafting, revising, and polishing. These stages are naturally recursive and overlapping; however, it's easiest to discuss them one at a time:

Step One: Planning

During the planning phase, writers gather materials and/or information to prepare to write. Here are some common planning activities for police officers:

- Driving to a crime scene, interviewing victims, complainants, and/or witnesses; examining a vehicle or residence for evidence; taking notes; determining a crime classification.

- Reading the departmental bylaws or union contract and taking notes of relevant sections; meeting with a union representative to discuss concerns and confirm procedures for filing a grievance; analyzing successful grievance files for content choices, organizational pattern, and overall tone.
- Meeting with school, city, and/or county officials to learn differing perspectives on a local problem, brainstorming possible solutions with each group, and reporting possible solutions to a shift supervisor; learning the solution the supervisor favors and why.
- Examining previous year-end reports or policy statements so the overall format, individual sections, and basic content are clear to the writer; taking notes in preparation for writing the current report or a new policy.
- Reading the guidelines for a local award or a national grant application, making a copy of the guidelines for a colleague or two and talking them over, creating a list of key points to include in the application; thinking about the grant or award application during off-duty hours at odd moments, like mowing the backyard or driving on the freeway.
- Checking the personnel file of an incompetent officer, cross-referencing attendance records and previous violations with police policy/procedures, talking with his/her previous shift supervisor.

In the long run, all of these planning strategies are designed to save the police officer's time. How much time do you think each strategy would take, and why are they all a good use of time? Which strategies do you believe police officers may naturally do at work, and which strategies might need to be learned? Why might each strategy ultimately save time in the long run? How do you think the planning strategies compare to the planning strategies that promote successful writing in academic or other professional settings?

Looking Back

Reconsider Scenario #2: A Promotion Request. What kinds of planning activities do you think the sergeant completed to create her resume and application letter?

Looking Back

Reconsider Scenario #5: A Directive. Did the lieutenant complete any planning activity before writing? Why? What planning activities might have been appropriate?

Step Two: Drafting

During the drafting stage, writers get their ideas down on paper. To be as efficient as possible, they often do the following:

- Create start-up rituals, such as clearing workspace, finishing smaller tasks, or making a fresh pot of coffee.

- Be aware of personal preferences: composing at the keyboard or by hand, using a #2 pencil or felt-tip marker, or writing in the morning or afternoon.
- Accept and adapt for workplace realities: limited time, frequent interruptions, noisy environment, shared clerical/computer support.
- Draft ASAP when memory plays a key role: committee minutes, police reports, and summaries of meetings, hearings, or telephone calls.
- Get ideas down quickly, without concern for overall organization, visual impact, or writer's tone.
- Know writing repertoires. Cadets and patrol officers write primarily police reports. As police reports become a more familiar format or *genre* (see Chapter Five), the drafting will automatically become faster and more efficient. On the other hand, ranked officers tend to write administrative documents. In large departments, ranked officers play highly specialized roles, so they write fewer kinds of documents; in contrast, ranked officers in smaller departments play broader roles, so they tend to write more kinds of documents. Like cadets and patrol officers, ranked officers draft more efficiently when they are familiar with the kinds of documents they write.
- Avoid at all costs: over editing prematurely, procrastinating on important documents, writing in anger, devoting excessive time, space, and/or energy to background information, writing complex/unfamiliar documents in one sitting.

These drafting strategies are designed to streamline the writing process. They encourage busy police officers to know and/or accept their own writing habits, repertoires, and workplace environments, so they can get ideas down on paper or the computer screen in the most efficient manner possible. Which strategies do you believe police officers may naturally do at work, and which strategies might need to be learned? How long would each strategy take, but how would the strategy ultimately save time in the long run? How do the drafting strategies compare to the drafting strategies that promote successful writing in academic or other professional settings?

Step Three: Revising

During revision, writers gain sufficient critical distance from their first drafts for a meaningful, but efficient, self-assessment—an assessment ensuring their work is as professional, persuasive, and reader-focused as possible. Effective writers know that revision takes time, but they wisely recognize that it is time better spent than doing damage control later—regardless of whether the audience is internal or external. Here are some common revision strategies for police officers:

- Double checking probable cause, case classification, and officer procedure in police reports; adding content to ensure that any reader—county prosecutor, defense attorney, and/or court official—would not call the report or the investigation, itself, into question (and waste time later).
- Ensuring an objective stance in reports by eliminating sarcastic or subjective language or adding concrete details and appropriate tone (see Chapter Five for a full discussion).
- Submitting a report for initial approval by the shift supervisor; making any change the supervisor proposes.

- Locating and underlining the articulated purpose of a document; deciding if its placement (beginning, middle, or end of the document) is reader-focused and, if necessary, making adjustments (see Chapter Seven for a full discussion).
- Re-conceptualizing the document to improve visual impact: check margins, add headings, include bulleted/indented lists, monitor "white space," and condense to one page, if possible (see Appendix C for a list of ten strategies).
- Asking a peer colleague to be a "second reader" by (a) reading a document and (b) explaining its purpose or message; truly listening to the colleague and avoiding defensive oral explanations ("This is what I meant to say; can't you see that?"); making necessary additions/deletions to address the colleague's concerns.
- Asking a friend or family member to serve as a "second reader" for an outside or "civilian perspective" (when such a perspective would be helpful).
- Putting the document aside for twenty minutes, an hour, or a day (depending on time constraints); printing a clean copy and then reading it from start to finish with fresh eyes while making notes in the margins.
- Circling effective sections; analyzing why they are effective and determining how the other sections might be enhanced using similar strategies.
- Examining proportionality: Does the heart or gist of the message take the most space in the document, or does background information dominate?

These revision strategies are designed to help busy police officers create the most effective document possible. Notice that most strategies prompt writers to gain a little distance so they are better able to reconsider purpose, audience, and/or overall tone. How much time would any of these strategies require? Which strategies do you believe police officers may naturally do at work, and which strategies might need to be learned? How long would each strategy take, but how would the strategy ultimately save time in the long run? How do these revision strategies compare to the revision strategies that promote successful writing in academic and other professional settings?

Looking Back

Reconsider Table 1.1: Six Circumstances. If a parade route suddenly changes (Bullet #4), writing time would be short but writing quality would be crucial. What kind of document would ensure appropriate staffing along the parade route? What quick revision activity would help to ensure that directions are clear?

Looking Back

Reconsider the common planning and drafting activities. In your opinion, would any of these activities work well during revision? Why? Defend your position by imagining a set of circumstances a police department might face; what kind of document would the circumstances prompt, and how would the document be enhanced with the activity you propose?

Step Four: Polishing

Before distribution, effective writers take the time to edit or polish. Here are some typical strategies:

- Confirming the correct spelling of names/addresses.
- Printing a clean copy and reading the document aloud to check for awkward or unclear phrasing.
- Using spell/grammar checks.
- Condensing sentence structure (see Chapter Three).
- Checking comma usage and other punctuation marks (see Chapter Two)
- Eliminating "spillage" (a few lines of text or a signature block spilling onto the top of the last page) by adjusting margins or print size.

These strategies are all designed to help police officers put the finishing touches on a document. Which strategies do you believe police officers may naturally do at work, and which strategies might need to be learned? How long would each strategy take, but how would the strategy ultimately save time in the long run? How do the polishing strategies compare to the polishing strategies that promote successful writing in academic or other professional settings?

Looking Back

Reconsider the idea of Writing as a Process in light of your own writing practices and then answer the following questions:

- What are your writing processes? Does your process vary from one document to the next; if yes, what influences your process? Is it time available, document familiarity/complexity, or a combination of both?
- What strategies do you use to enhance planning, drafting, revision, and polishing? How much time does each strategy take and does it ultimately save time in the long run? How do you know the strategies are effective?
- What could you do to enhance your writing processes? How will you balance writing processes with time constraints?
- Why do you think most inexperienced writers tackle most writing tasks in the same way, typically sitting down cold and writing from start to finish with nothing more than a quick spell/grammar check?

Writing as a Developmental Skill

Effective writers tend to agree that writing is a developmental skill. In other words, there is no writing vaccination or immunization: no single course, textbook, teacher, or event has the power to eliminate all writing woes or to promote writing competence. Instead, writing growth takes place gradually over time, and most effective writers believe that they are constantly growing as writers. For example, an effective writer would never claim, "I earned an 'A' in 12th grade English (or ENG 101); what else do I have to learn?"

What kinds of activities are likely to promote long-term writing growth across all disciplines and fields? Most people generally agree that reading is a basic foundation and that it's essential to practice writing too. In a recent study at Harvard University, however, Nancy Sommers and Laura Saltz found that a positive attitude about writing is also crucial. In particular, they found that students grow the most as writers when they do the following:

- Believe that writing is an important activity allowing a person to engage with the world.
- Understand they have a lot to learn about writing and so are receptive to constructive criticism.
- Recognize that writing tasks may differ, but they are all somehow connected (and so what is learned in one writing activity might be helpful in the next and the next and the next).

If police officers want to be truly excellent writers, they must have a positive attitude too. They must see value in the written word, they must be open to constructive criticism, and they must see themselves as constantly growing as writers.

Chapter Review

Written communication is linked to leadership. It has the power to promote positive or negative change:

- Build or break a writer's self-image.
- Enhance or eradicate pubic relations.
- Promote or impede policies and procedures.
- Increase or annihilate *esprit de corps*.

Effective writers are not born that way; they learn attitudes and behaviors that render them both efficient and effective.

- They know that any written document is a response to a specific set of circumstances. To respond effectively, the writer must analyze the Big Picture by taking into consideration purpose, audience, writer/audience relationship, and form/genre.
- They know that writing is a process with four overlapping stages: planning, drafting, revising, editing. They know that these stages overlap and that they take less time when the writer is familiar with the document at hand.
- They understand that writing is a developmental skill.

For Discussion

1. Do you define yourself as a writer? Why?
2. Name a document you have recently read that promoted negative or positive change. Did it build or break the writer's self image? Did it enhance or eradicate PR? Did it promote or impede policies/programs? Did it increase or annihilate *esprit de corps*? Explain.
3. Name the last three non-school related documents you have written. What were the circumstances that prompted you to write? What was the Big Picture? Identify the purpose, audience, writer/audience relationship and form/genre for each of the three documents.
4. What is your writing process? Do you have specific strategies or rituals for planning, drafting, revising and polishing? If yes, what are they? If no, why not? How do you balance writing process and time constraints?
5. Imagine that you are writing the following documents: a police report for an arson investigation, a year-end report for traffic accidents, and a general order regarding dress codes. What planning activities would be necessary before drafting could begin? What drafting, revision, and polishing strategies would you use?

Test Yourself

Practice Set #1.1

Read the memos written by Sergeant Scott Brown of the Germantown Police Department and Sergeant Donald Claar of the Delaware Police Department. Then answer the questions that follow.

DATE

To: Terri Zimmerman
FR: Scott Brown, Sergeant
RE: German Township Police Records

German Township Police Department has recently signed a contract for dispatching services with our communication center. The contract stipulates that we will make available to the GTPD (a) records from our CAD/MIS system and (b) two logs from the previous month.

I am putting you in charge of this new monthly detail. First, you have a vast knowledge of the CAD system. Second, you are consistently accurate and reliable in your record keeping. Third, I am confident you would serve as a professional and cooperative GPD/GTPD liaison. As you know, your next performance evaluation will take place next January; by that time, you will have been responsible for this task for almost six months, and it will surely reflect well in your write-up.

If you have questions about the new GTPD contract, please let me know. Otherwise, I would like implementation to begin on October 6 and continue thereafter on the first Monday of each month.

DATE

To: Chief of Police
Fr: Sergeant Donald Claar
RE: Mason Avenue Traffic Solution

For many years, an ongoing and growing traffic problem has existed on Mason Avenue, specifically during the hours prior to the start and close of the Smith Elementary School. In response, I have surveyed Mason Avenue (See Diagram #1) and investigated three possible solutions. As this letter makes clear, I recommend the third option.

The first solution is to ignore the problem. After all, the inconvenience and congestion lasts for about forty-five minutes in the morning and afternoon, and the MPD could continue to field citizen complaints and write parking tickets. The second solution (See Diagram #2) is to widen the street adjacent to the school to create an additional pick-up and drop-off area. This solution would require moving at least two utility poles, the planting strip, and a side-walk, but it would create an additional five feet of road sufficient to allow traffic to move freely in both directions. The third solution (see Diagram #3) is to make Mason Avenue a one-way street (westbound) with no-stopping, standing, or parking signage on the north side of the street. This approach would allow for a pick-up area on the north side of the street and unrestricted westbound traffic flow.

I recommend the third option for several reasons. First of all, the first option creates a safe-ty hazard and the second option is cost prohibitive. In short, there are serious problems asso-ciated with both of the first two options. Second, the third option resolves the traffic prob-lem (parents may safely and legally pick up/drop off their children), while causing minimal inconvenience to Mason Street residents (drive time from the furthest Mason Avenue resi-dence back to North Liberty is 1.5 minutes). Most importantly, however, the implementa-tion of this change is relatively simple; it involves temporary signage alerting motorists of a change in traffic patterns and permanent signage for the north side of the street.

Thank you for your consideration. If you have questions, please do not hesitate to ask.

Questions

1. What is the Big Picture for each document?
2. What leadership intentions does each writer hope to achieve by writing?
3. What planning, drafting, revising, and polishing strategies do you believe each writer used?

Practice Set #1.2

Read the two versions of the memo written by Sergeant John Crowell of the Montgomery Police Department and then answer the questions that follow.

Original Version

Dear Mr. Smith:

I received your letter concerning your property. It is currently secured in our property room under #5528. The items include a Kentucky ID, several credit cards, a cell phone, and a checkbook. These items can remain here until your sentence is complete. Normally, items secured in our property room require the owner to retrieve them in person, as we must account for all items. Under special circumstances, items could be turned over to a parent or other relative that you designate.

If you wish for these items to remain in our property room until your release, then there is no reason to respond to this letter.

If there is a relative that you wish to have pick up the property, then please send me their name and phone number. I can make arrangements to have them sign in person for the property.

Respectfully,

John Crowell, Sergeant
Montgomery Police Department

Revised Version

Dear Mr. Smith:

I received your letter concerning your property. It is currently secured in our property room under #5528 and includes the following: a Kentucky ID card, several credit cards, a cell phone, and a check book. Normally, secured items require that the owner retrieve them in person, as we must account for all items; however, these items could be turned over to a parent or other relative, under special circumstances. This policy is in place for your protection. It ensures the privacy of individuals incarcerated by the MPD, as well as the safekeeping and handling of their personal property.

If you wish to have a family member pick up your personal belongings, please send me the person's name and phone number, and I will make arrangements. If you wish for your personal property items to remain in our property room until your release, there is no need to respond to this letter.

Respectfully,

John Crowell, Sergeant
Montgomery Police Department

Questions

1. What is the Big Picture of this document? What are the purpose, audience, and format? Do you think the letter accomplished the writer's leadership goal?

2. What planning activities do you believe the writer completed to write the letter? How long do you think it took him to draft the original version? What revision strategies do you think he used to revise? Did he properly edit the letter before mailing? Most importantly, do you think that the letter accomplished the writer's leadership goals?

3. What is the difference between the original and revised versions? Do you think that the revised version is more effective? Is it more likely to promote positive change? Does it build self-image? Does it enhance PR? Does it promote policy or procedure? Does it increase *esprit de corps*? Given the audience, do these questions matter? Why? Be prepared to defend your position.

Practice Set #1.3

Here are three sets of circumstances prompting a police report: Assuming that writing is a process, what kinds of planning activities would be necessary for each set of circumstances? Be sure to include case classification and probable cause.

- Two residents have complained about a block parties in a residential neighborhood.
- A woman calls to say that she was beaten by her ex-boyfriend.
- Students at a local university have staged a protest rally against a KKK speaker.

Practice Set #1.4

A newspaper plans to publish press releases with the titles listed below. What set of circumstances would prompt each press release? Imagine hypothetical circumstances beyond what the titles suggest. In other words, imagine the Big Picture. If the editor asked YOU to write the press releases, what leadership intentions would be accomplished? More specifically, would you be building self-image, enhancing PR, promoting policies/procedures, and/or increasing esprit de corps?

- Officer Honored for Saving Local First Grader
- Retirement Party Organized for Police Chief Bennet
- Gang-Related Arrest Made

MyCompLab—Optional Exercises and Activities

As the homepage shows, MyCompLab is divided into three sections: Grammar, Writing, and Research. Under Writing, complete the following Writing Process activities:

1. Click "Writing Process Exercises."

    • Read Introduction to Prewriting and Introduction to Planning. Select Questioning under Prewriting and then complete this activity using a writing activity assigned in class. As you answer, consider how questions relate to the Big Picture concept.

    • Read Introduction to Drafting and Introduction to Revision. Select Improving Focus and Structure and Speaking to Your Audience. Analyze the strategies in these exercises and consider their relevance to police. Could strategies be adapted to suite the writing needs of a police officer?' Be prepared to defend your answers in small groups, class discussion, or written form, as your instructor requests.

    • Read Introduction to Finishing. Select Checking Voice and Proofreading for Grammar Errors. Then complete all activities as the final stage of a paper assigned by your instructor before reflecting: Did the strategies expand your writing process in meaningful ways? Why or why not? Over time, how might these strategies help you to grow and develop as a writer?

2. Click "Writing Video Tutorials." Review the five "Office Hours Series" videos, select one, and then write a one-page response, explaining its applicability to police writing to an audience of your choice.

CHAPTER TWO

PUTTING GRAMMAR IN ITS PLACE

My writing is well organized and prepared in a professional way. It relies on factual information and events. When a problem exists, it offers a recommendation. Even when the general tone is negative, it offers a positive suggestion or reinforcement.

Sergeant Jennifer Wuertz
Worthington Division of Police
Worthington, Ohio

Leadership Objectives

- To identify and correct the "Top Ten" errors most commonly found in police documents.
- To increase confidence in the area of grammar/usage and, in turn, professional self-image; to foster the same in colleagues department wide.

Assess Yourself

Ask yourself the following questions:

- Has your credibility ever been compromised because of grammar mistakes?
- A writer can substitute *myself* in place of *me* and *I*, right?
- Do readers notice misplaced commas in your written work? Do you think they are aware of your confusion over word pairs, like *effect* and *affect* or *complement* and *compliment*?
- By using the "all caps" key, is it possible for a writer to camouflage a lack of knowledge over capitalization rules?
- Does spell or grammar check have the power to catch all mistakes?
- Do you waste time worrying about grammar and usage conventions?

The *Blue Guide* continues with what police officers often say is their most pressing written communication concern: grammar and usage. Is grammar and usage the most complex issue? No. Is it truly the most important? Maybe not. Even so, it is crucial to address grammar and usage because most police officers admit they lack professional confidence in this area. They recall former English teachers circling mistakes on their homework and formal papers but to no avail; the rules didn't sink in. This fact may not have been perceived as a problem back in school, but it is now, working in the field of law enforcement. First of all, police officers have very busy schedules, and so their writing time is too often scarce. As a result, they have far better ways to spend their limited time and energy than worrying over pesky grammar and usage conventions. Secondly, grammar and usage errors do have the potential of undermining a writer's credibility, thus reducing the Power of the Pen.

Like any leadership challenge, the best approach to tackling grammar and usage is a proactive one, and so what follows in this chapter is a highly focused list of the "Top Ten" grammar and usage errors police officers are most likely to make. Each error is identified as a *Focused Correction Area* (FCA). An FCA identifies solely one error, explains the correct rule, and then illustrates it using sample sentences derived from actual police documents.

The FCAs found in The *Blue Guide* will, most obviously, help police officers correct common grammar and usage errors found in their own written communication, thus increasing confidence while simultaneously enhancing professional self-image and increasing the Power of the Pen. Less obviously, however, the FCAs are designed to help police officers be writing teachers and evaluators of their peers' and subordinates' written work. In other words, police officers familiar with the "Top Ten" are better equipped to raise the writing standards of their police departments too.

"TOP TEN" FCAS FOR POLICE OFFICERS

FCA #1: Numbers

Remember: "Spell out" numbers comprised of one or two words (ten, twenty-four, two hundred, one billion), unless they are combined with an abbreviation or symbol.
Do not follow numbers with digits in parentheses.

Examples:

The Billsport Police Department needs twenty new squad cars.
Records show that over eight hundred drug arrests took place last year.
His tour of duty will last the customary eight hours.
The workshop will begin at 8:00 AM and costs $100.00.
Approximately 68% of the arrests are related to alcohol.

Remember: Write as numerical digits numbers comprised of three or more words (101, 328, 2003, 4,289, 3.6), unless they are the first words of a sentence.

Examples:
The total number far exceeds the 250-officer quota.
We contacted 129 local organizations to participate in Toys for Tots.
His blood-alcohol level was 1.2.
Two hundred fifty-six officers attended the conference.
Nineteen forty-eight was the year that Chief Smith began his tenure.

FCA #2: Comma after Introductory Elements

Remember: Use a comma after introductory elements in sentences.

Examples:

At 9:00 PM, the witness arrived and began the interview.
If Encryption fails, the message will show "key fail."
As we agreed last November, the meeting will take place Tuesday.
Once a year, I will conduct a complete inspection.
Bill, I know that you are capable of better job performance.
Upon arrival, the witness indicated that Joshua had been there.
On December 13 at 2:00 PM, I met with Sergeant Strickler.
Obviously, the V-Day form must be submitted on time.
However, Officer Erickson denied the accusation.
If you have questions, please don't hesitate to ask me.

FCA #3: Possessive Nouns

Remember: When the noun is singular, add an apostrophe and then an "s."

Examples:

The officer's uniform was pressed and clean.
The victim's face was bruised and scarred.
The committee's report was carefully prepared.
Mr. Jones's property was vandalized.

Looking Back

Consider a revision of the four examples:

> Chief Anderson, the officer's uniform was pressed and clean.
> On April 5, the victim's face was bruised and scarred.
> Despite contrary claims, the committee's report was carefully prepared.
> Last month, Mr. Jones's property was vandalized.

Are the added commas correct? Why?

Remember: When the noun is plural and ends with an "s," add only an apostrophe. If the noun is plural and doesn't end with "s" (men, deer, children), add an apostrophe and then an "s."

Examples:

The officers' uniforms were pressed and clean.

The victims' faces were bruised and scarred.

The committees' reports were carefully prepared.

The Joneses' (Mr. Jones and his children's) property was vandalized.

The children's tree fort was demolished.

The deer's hindquarters were sticking through the windshield.

Remember: When two nouns show possession of the same object(s), place an apostrophe after the second noun. When they show possession of different objects, place an apostrophe after both nouns.

Examples:

Officer Smith and Officer Bilt's squad car was demolished.

Officer Smith's and Officer Bilt's squad cars were both demolished.

Jo and Al's parents arrived at the station (Jo and Al are siblings).

Jo's and Al's parents all arrived at the station (Jo and Al aren't siblings).

Remember: Do not add apostrophes to possessive pronouns: mine, yours, her/hers/his/its, ours, yours, theirs.

Examples:

The mistake was mine.

Yours truly,

The award was hers (or his).

The gun was broken, its trigger faulty.

The honor was yours.

The pride was theirs.

FCA #4: Me, Myself, and I

Remember: Use "myself" (and the other reflexive pronouns, such as yourself, him/herself, ourselves, yourselves, and themselves) for solely two reasons: (1) to show emphasis and (2) to complement reflexive verbs.

Examples:

I told him, myself, that he was suspended.

He, himself, must answer the question.

I looked at myself in the mirror.

He shot himself in the foot.

Looking Back

Consider a revision of the second example: He, himself, must answer the committee's question. Explain why an apostrophe is needed. How would the apostrophe change if there were two committees asking the same questions or two committees asking their own questions?

Remember: Do not use "myself" as the subject or object of a phrase or sentence, even if it "sounds right."

Examples:

Incorrect: Officer Brownstone and myself took the initiative
Correct: Officer Brownstone and I took the initiative.

Incorrect: Sergeant Tovar and myself agreed to complete the task.
Correct: Sergeant Tovar and I agreed to complete the task.

Incorrect: Nobody, but myself, knows the truth.
Correct: Nobody, but me, knows the truth.

Incorrect: Give the keys to Deputy Green or myself.
Correct: Give the keys to Deputy Green or me.

Incorrect: Please contact Officer Jelt or myself.
Correct: Please contact Officer Jelt or me.

FCA #5: Job Titles

Remember: Capitalize job titles when they are included as part of the person's first and/or last name.

Examples:

The committee gave Deputy Semula the award this year.
I can confirm that Dispatcher Frank Wilcox arrived on time.
Do you agree that Detective Bob will be the DARE officer?
By 8:00, Chief Tanski will arrive for the press conference.

Looking Back

Circle the right answer—me, myself, or I—in the following sentences:

The committee gave the award to Deputy Semula and me/myself this year.
I can confirm that Dispatcher Frank Wilcox arrived on time with me/myself.
Do you agree that Detective Bob and myself/I will be the DARE officers?
By 8:00, Chief Tanski and myself/I will arrive for the press conference.

What FCA provides the rationale for the use of *me, myself, and I*?

Remember: Do not capitalize job titles when they are not "attached" to the person's first and/or last name.

Examples:

The committee gave the deputy the award this year.
I can confirm that the dispatcher arrived on time.
Do you agree that the detective will be the DARE officer?
By 8:00, the chief will arrive for the press conference.

Note: If department protocol requires capitalization, determine at what rank it begins, and be consistent. In nearly all police departments, "the Chief" is capitalized. However, see the exception in the next rule.

Remember: Do not capitalize job titles when referring to groups of individuals.

Examples:

The deputies were given the award this year.
The dispatchers arrived on time.
The detectives will serve as the DARE officers.
The chiefs will arrive by 8:00 AM for the press conference.

Looking Back

Police officers intuitively know to write the numerical digit for the phrase, "8:00 AM," but what is the rule?

FCA #6: Commas before Conjunctions ("And," "But," and "Or")

> **Remember:** Place a comma before "and" and "or" when three or more items are listed in a series, or omit the comma: the choice is yours, but be consistent!

Examples:

The locker was filled with guns, ammunition, and file folders.
The locker was filled with guns, ammunition and file folders.
The office equipment includes computers, cell phones, or faxes.
The office equipment includes computers, cell phones or faxes.

> **Remember:** Place a comma before "and," "but," and "or" when the sentence is comprised of two independent clauses (that is, when the two "sides" of the sentence are both complete sentences and can, therefore, "stand alone").

Examples:

The officer walked to the door, and she opened it quickly.
The officer offered assistance to the victim, but he refused.
The deputies arrived late, but they accomplished their goals.

> **Remember:** Do not place a comma before "and," "but," and "or" when the sentence is comprised of an independent clause and a dependent clause (one that is not a complete sentence and, therefore, can not stand alone).

Examples:

The officer walked to the door and opened it quickly.
The officer offered assistance to the victim but refused.
The deputies arrived late but accomplished their goals.

> ### Looking Back
>
> Why aren't the job titles capitalized in the previous sentences? What FCA explains the rule?

FCA #7: Noun/Pronoun Agreement

> **Remember:** Use masculine and feminine pronouns when referring to a specific person.

Examples:

If Officer Paul Strome wants to apply, he should do so.
If Officer Sally Backus wants to apply, she should do so.

Looking Back

Notice the commas in the previous two examples. What FCA explains why a comma is needed?

Remember: Do not use "they" or "their" to refer to one person. Instead, use pronoun pairs, revise the sentence to reflect more than one person, or omit the pronoun.

Examples:

If a civilian would like to apply, she/he should do so.
If civilians would like to apply, they should do so.
Civilians interested in applying should do so.

A drug user will be agitated, his/her behavior unpredictable.
Drug users will be agitated, their behavior unpredictable.
Drug users will be agitated and exhibit unpredictable behaviors.

Remember: Do not use "they" or "their" in conjunction with "anyone" or "someone." Instead, use pronoun pairs, revise the sentence to reflect more than one person, or omit the pronoun.

Examples:

Officers will not wait for someone while she/he is being treated.
Officers will not wait for victims while they are being treated.
Officers will not wait for anyone being treated.

Remember: Use a singular pronoun in junction with a committee, department, or other single entity, even though it is comprised of many members. Use a plural pronoun when referring to committee members.

Examples:

The committee concluded in its report that the evidence is faulty.
Committee members concluded in their report that the evidence is faulty.

Does the Adson Police Department review its policies?

Do Adson police administrators review their policies?

The staff reneged on its offer.

Staff members reneged on their offer.

FCA #8: Sexist Language

Remember: Replace sexist words with gender-neutral ones.

Examples:

Incorrect: *Policemen must have integrity and honor.*

Correct: *Police officers must have integrity and honor.*

Incorrect: *Personnel files should include atta boys.*

Correct: *Personnel files should include commendations.*

Incorrect: *Officers had been assigned to three-man teams.*

Correct: *Officers had been assigned to three-person teams.*

Incorrect: *The HPD will participate in manning the booth.*

Correct: *The HPD will participate in staffing the booth.*

Incorrect: *Before an officer checks out, he should complete all paperwork.*

Correct: *Before officers check out, they should complete all paperwork.*

FCA #9: Quotation Marks

Remember: Use quotation marks to quote directly a person's actual words. Notice the "speech tags" (followed by a comma) that begin each quoted line.

Examples:

Mr. Cline clearly stated, "I was home from midnight until 2:00 AM last night."

Officer Simmons shouted, "Put down your weapon!"

Deputy Thompson asked, "Did you return to school after your lunch hour?"

I responded, "Open the door."

Remember: Place the end punctuation mark within the quotations.

Examples:

The name of the workshop is "Tactical Strategies for the Year 2003."

The officer shouted, "Stop in the name of the law!"

The officer shouted, "Stop in the name of the law!" before proceeding.
The defendant was found "not guilty," at least in the eyes of the jury.

Looking Back

Consider this sentence: The officer shouted. Why not capitalize the "'o'" in officer? What if the officer's last name was included in the statement? Would the "d" in defendant be capitalized? Why?

FCA #10: Confusing Pairs of Words

Remember: Using the incorrect word is one of the most common usage mistakes in police writing, and it's considered one of the most serious too. Because literally dozens of easily confused word pairs exist, it is impossible to target each and every one. However, the following list provides a good start. Each word pair includes concrete definitions and sample sentences.

---

1. **Accept/Except.** **Accept** is a verb meaning to receive, approve, or agree: *Sergeant Smith accepts your resignation.* **Except** is a preposition meaning excluding or only. *The entire squad will participate, except for Lieutenant Wilson.*

2. **Access/Excess. Access** is a noun referring to an ability to enter or approach. *Patrol officers now have access to new technology.* **Excess** is an adjective meaning overabundance. *Excess use of overtime is prohibited.*

3. **Affect/Effect. Affect** is a verb meaning to influence. *The reprimand positively affected the officers because they changed their behavior.* **Effect** is a noun meaning outcome. *Regardless of procedure, the end result, or effect, is the same.*

4. **All Ready/Already. All ready** is an adjective meaning fully prepared. *The officers are all ready for the investigation.* **Already** is an adverb meaning previously or by this time. *The mayor had already signed the papers.*

5. **All Together/Altogether. All together** means everyone or as a group. *By working all together, the squadron members achieved their goal.* **Altogether** is an adverb meaning thoroughly, in all, or all told. *The training program has been altogether revamped.*

6. **Among/Between. Among** is a preposition used when referring to three or more people or entities. *Among the three candidates, Officer Jones is the most qualified.* **Between** is a preposition used when referring to two people or entities. *We can accomplish more by dividing responsibilities between the APD and the PDP.*

7. **Bad/Badly. Bad** is a noun describing a person, place, thing, or idea. *The officer's behavior was bad.* **Badly** is an adverb meaning poorly. *The investigation went badly.*

8. **Compliment/Complement. Compliment** is a verb or noun designed to commend or flatter. *The chief complimented the sergeants on their well-run shifts.* **Complement** is a noun referring to items that match or enhance. *Trooper Torreano's expertise perfectly complements his partner's.*

9. **Criterion/Criteria. Criterion** is a singular noun referring to a standard or trait. *The most important criterion is leadership ability.* **Criteria** is the plural form of the same word. *The most important criteria are leadership ability and professional expertise.*

10. **Farther/Further. Farther** is an adverb referring to physical distance. *The suspect took two steps farther and then disappeared into the building.* **Further** is an adverb referring to a greater degree or extent. *I will discuss this matter no further.*

11. **Fewer/Less. Fewer** is an adjective indicating a smaller number of individuals or things that can be individually counted. *The chief believes that fewer problems will arise with the second approach.* Less is an adjective indicating a smaller portion or quantity that can't be counted. By reducing speed, motorists use less gas and promote highway safety.

12. **Good/Well. Good** is an adjective describing a person, place, thing, or idea. *The police report is a good example of Officer Jenkin's strong investigative skills.* **Well** is an adverb describing how something was done. *Officer Jenkin writes well.*

13. **Stationary/Stationery. Stationary** is an adjective referring to an unmoving object. *The stationary bicycle is a valuable piece of exercise equipment for the work-out room.* **Stationery** is a noun referring to writing paper. *We have updated the GPD letterhead stationery to reflect the recently approved mission statement.*

14. **Than/Then. Than** is a conjunction or preposition used in comparisons. *Our standards are higher than theirs.* **Then** is an adverb referring to time. *I observed the suspect talking on the phone and then exiting the telephone booth.*

15. **Whose/Who's. Whose** is a possessive pronoun. *Chief Beltnick wants to know whose uniform has been left in the locker room.* **Who's** is a contraction meaning who is. *Who's (who is) going to attend The Annual Police Ball?*

Chapter Review

Grammar and usage may not be the most complex writing issue that police officers face; however, it is an important one. Improving grammar/usage increases confidence, and it enhances professional self-image.

The "Top Ten" errors found in police documents include the following: (1) numbers, (2) comma after introductory elements, (3) possessive nouns, (4) me, myself, & I, (5) capitalization (job titles), (6) comma before conjunctions, (7) noun/pronoun agreement, (8) sexist language, and (9) quotation marks & end punctuation marks, and (10) easily confused words).

For Discussion

1. Do you notice grammar and usage mistakes in the media, including TV ads, billboards, and newspapers print? Give some examples. Do the mistakes bother you or someone you know?
2. What grammar rules confuse you? If the answer is "comma rules," can you clarify which one(s)?
3. Has your credibility ever been undermined by a grammar/usage mistake? What was the document? What was the mistake? What happened? Share the story.
4. Has anyone ever embarrassed you over a grammar or usage mistake by circling it in red pen or posting it in a public place? How did this make you feel? Do you recommend this strategy?
5. What are effective approaches for teaching others who struggle with grammar and usage conventions? Why do you think it would work?
6. Would you be a more efficient and confident writer if you had a better understanding grammar and usage? Why or why not?

Test Yourself

Practice Set #2.1

Here are twenty sentences taken directly from actual police documents. Read them carefully and correct the error found in each one. Identify the FCA.

1. A complaint was received regarding parking in the 200 block of Vanderville Road, and the drive to Vanderville Park.
2. Kevin you were scheduled to work from 1800-600 hours on August 25.
3. We currently have 17 sworn officers in this department.
4. The jail had twelve officers (six male/six female), but we were undermanned.
5. At that time we started providing paramedic services.
6. We contacted your dispatcher and she put me on a three-way call to PO Smitters.
7. The extra manpower—one or two officers—will be used primarily on weekends.
8. Please contact Sergeant Simmons or myself.
9. If I can be of further assistance to you feel free to contact me at the office.
10. You have 14 days from today to contact me.
11. No vulgar or inappropriate pictures will be posted were the public will see them.
12. As I let technicians into the phone room they are amazed at its set up.
13. On behalf of the BPD, I'm writing to thank you for donating K-9 Lennys burial stone.
14. While these subjects were being detained, a fellow officer returned to the retirement complex and noticed that a construction trailer had been broken into and set on fire.
15. Al is trying to move all equipment out of the room, but fears it will happen soon.

16. This policy replaces any former written policy, or verbal authorization that deviates from this document.
17. I recognize my Badge to be a symbol of Public Faith.
18. Each unit is responsible for checking "hot spots" assigned to them.
19. She walked to the hall and allowed the crew to do there job.
20. I would like to submit Benjamin Brothers for a recognition award.

Practice Set #2.2

Here are twenty sentences taken directly from actual police documents. Read them carefully and correct the error found in each one. Identify the FCA.

1. I am a "partially qualified person".
2. One of Toms most impressive features is his integrity.
3. I would like to recommend the following TPD for recognition.
4. Any officer violating this directive shall have his personal phone privileges revoked.
5. Give your ideas to Lieutenant Morey or myself.
6. Training for the month included two officers attending a class entitled "Working with People with Mental Illness in the Criminal Justice System".
7. To date, we have lost seven (7) officers this year.
8. If a vendor has specific questions, refer them to the on-duty supervisor.
9. On-duty Officers were dispatched to meet with residents regarding their concerns.
10. The officer played a major role in the cities' emergency plan.
11. The complaint letter noted that the officer was out right sarcastic.
12. Do not cite the accused for the next business day of the court unless they have been committed to the county jail.
13. The only notation was made when LEADS called our radio room, and attempted to talk to our personnel through the process of rebooting the system.
14. The officer advised that he does not feel that it is an "injury".
15. However, the most obvious advantage is the length of time a defendant would receive in the Federal Courts.
16. Some examples may include serial abductions or gang fights effecting the school.
17. She rarely takes off sick, and arrives to work on time.
18. Effective today, all units shall submit the following list to Captain Davenports office.
19. In order to rectify this situation it is imperative that all supervisors monitor the number of vacation days used.
20. You can accomplish this goal by meeting with Captain Colbertson or myself.

Practice Set #2.3

Here are twenty sentences taken directly from actual police documents. Read them carefully and correct the error found in each one. Identify the FCA.

1. It was farther suggested that invitations might include, but not be limited to, the members of the City Council, the County Commission, and the Civil Service Board.
2. We agreed their does seem to be less interaction among patrol officers.
3. The AFIS' server will be located at our station with one workstation in my unit.
4. Properly mark the container and it will be placed into the refrigerator.
5. The DPD formed a "Rapid Response Team", made up of specially trained officers.
6. On an average day the average citizen may use a credit card to make an internet transaction or order tickets for a ballgame over the telephone.
7. Please advice, if you have questions.
8. Patrol Office Daniels saw the vehicle with it's emergency flashers activated.
9. Despite my absence Detective Cohenna kept the section running well.
10. Trooper Trainor and myself anticipate continuing the proactive drug investigations.
11. The car was recovered on February 8th.
12. Credible information must suggest that a child was forcibly removed or intentionally lured away from their location.
13. Lieutenant Milner sent an email indicating that Night Shift was short a Dispatcher.
14. Johnson ran forward and caught up to the male by the North exit of the building.
15. It's nice to know we can look to you and your officer's for such assistance.
16. If a person takes the time to write a complaint letter, they must be very angry.
17. During his tenure, Bill has worked hundreds of hours with other Deputies and me.
18. The City Commission met to discuss their 2005 agenda items.
19. Obtain callers name, address, and phone number.
20. The Institute of Police Technology and Management will host a Police Internal Affairs course at their Jacksonville campus.

Practice Set #2.4

Read "The Spell Checker Poem" and circle the incorrect words.

> I have a spelling checker
> It came with my PC;
>
> It plainly marks four my revue
> Mistakes I cannot sea.
>
> I've run this poem threw it,
> I'm sure your pleased too no.
>
> Its letter perfect in its weigh
> My checker tolled me sew.

http://www.focusmagazine.org/wit/scp.htm (on February 18, 2006)

Rewrite the poem, using the correct forms of all words.

MyCompLab—Optional Exercises and Activities

As the homepage shows, MyCompLab is divided into three sections: Grammar, Writing, and Research. Under Grammar, complete the following activities.

- Click Grammar Diagnostics and complete Comprehensive Diagnostic I and/or II, as your instructor requests. Analyze your results. Do your most common mistakes correlate to the ten grammar/usage errors discussed in *The Blue Guide*? If not, what are your most common errors? How will you tackle them?
- Click ExerciseZone. Using your diagnostics results, locate the exercises most relevant for you and complete both basic/intermediate and intermediate/advanced exercises, as your instructor requests. Next, analyze two recent documents you have written, paying close attention for your most common errors.
- Click ESL ExerciseZone. Complete the exercises required by your instructor.
- Click Grammar Video Tutors. Compare the "Top 20 Grammar Errors" to the ten errors identified in *The Blue Guide*. What grammar/usage mistakes appear on both lists, and what rules don't? Watch any video associated with your diagnostics results and then do the same for the "Writing in Action Series." Be prepared in a small group or class discussion to explain how the videos enhance the FCAs found in *The Blue Guide* and the ExerciseZone in MyCompLab.
- Visit Web Links. Surf this section of MyCompLab for engaging and helpful Websites and then write a one-page document recommending a specific site for classmates. In your recommendation, be sure to identify the site in the introduction and provide a rationale with specific examples.

CHAPTER THREE

WRITING CONCISE SENTENCES

Effective written communication strengthens my credibility throughout my organization and within my area of supervision.

Sergeant Edward Depinet
Oregon Police Division
Oregon, Ohio

Leadership Objectives

- To identify and practice strategies for writing sentences that are clear, concise, and to the point.
- To increase confidence in the area of sentence structure and, in turn, professional self-image; to foster the same in colleagues department wide.

Assess Yourself

Ask yourself the following questions:

- Are your sentences long? Do they tend to run two, three, or four lines and often take up full paragraphs?
- Have superiors or teachers told you to cut passive voice from your writing?
- Have you been taught never to use first-person pronouns in writing? If yes, do you often rephrase in ways you would never actually do if you were talking with friends or family?
- Do you try to "sound like a cop" when you write?
- Do you believe that longer documents are better than shorter ones?
- Do you worry that you might cut crucial content if you condense your sentences?

The *Blue Guide* continues with a topic of universal importance to all police officers: being "clear, concise, and to the point." Do most police officers claim they value written communication demonstrating these three rhetorical features? The answer is a resounding yes. Do individual sentences of police officers, however, provide evidence of the same? The answer is an equally resounding no. In short, police documents are filled with wordy and sometimes even convoluted sentences, and it seriously detracts from the Power of the Pen. As a result, writing wordy sentences is a serious problem that all police officers must address. The question, of course, is how.

Like any leadership initiative, the best approach is a proactive one. As a logical starting point, consider why—despite strong verbal claims to the contrary—police documents tend to be wordy. First and perhaps most importantly, police officers compete linguistically with lawyers. In other words, it may be that police officers write *copspeak* because lawyers write legalese. Another related possibility is ego. Some police officers mistakenly believe the best way to "sound smart" is by lengthening written communication with verbose and overly formal sentences. Nothing, however, could be further from the truth. Still another factor may be lack of time. After all, it takes time to pare a sentence to its essence so that each word truly counts, and as *The Blue Guide* has emphasized, police officers tend to work under fairly severe time constraints. A final factor may stem directly from the very nature of police work. Police officers must be comprehensive in all aspects of their work, so they may worry that condensing sentences in written communication will eliminate content crucial to an investigation or situation at hand. As this chapter demonstrates, however, it is possible to be comprehensive and concise. To clarify, consider the following four sentence pairs. The first sentence in each pair comes directly from an actual police document; the second is a concise revision.

Sentence Pair #1

Original. In reference to the complaints made against Officer Jerry Burgess by the complainant Nancy Faldent, the following are the results of this investigation by myself as you requested.

Revised. As you requested, I have investigated Case #1234 against Officer Jerry Burgess. Here are the results.

Sentence Pair #2

Original. After having reviewed the proposed addition to the Code of Ordinances as regards the clear identification by number of every property, I have the following suggestions to add to this proposal.

Revised. I have reviewed the proposed addition to the Code of Ordinances and offer the following suggestions.

Sentence Pair #3

Original. The purpose of this letter is to establish department policy concerning request for an officer(s) of this department to accompany an individual to retrieve personal belongings or to act as a witness to the rendering of request for eviction or matters of this type (police escort).

Revised. This letter establishes policy for working as a police escort.

Sentence Pair #4

Original. Writing in a concise manner is something that I consistently strive to accomplish.

Revised. I strive to write concisely.

What is the difference between the first and second sentences in each of the four pairs? A quick analysis reveals the content is identical, and so crucial content has not been lost in the "condensing process." The first sentence pair introduces investigation results, the second pair proposes code changes, the third pair sets policy for police escorts, and the fourth pair makes a personal observation. Despite similarity in content, however, the second sentence in each pair is far more direct, concise, and to the point. How is that possible? What rhetorical strategies could help a police officer do the same, and how will the strategies enhance the Power of the Pen?

To answer these questions, keep reading. The five strategies that reduced word count in the four sentence pairs are demonstrated in this chapter and they are also "cop specific." They address the wordy rhetorical features typically found in police documents. These strategies include the following: (1) Dividing Long Sentences, (2) Eliminating Passive Voice, (3) Reducing Copspeak, (4) Addressing Repetition and Redundancy, and (5) Cutting Words "Here and There."

FIVE STRATEGIES FOR WRITING SENTENCES THAT ARE CLEAR, CONCISE, AND TO THE POINT

Strategy #1: Dividing Long Sentences

Police officers tend to write very long sentences. At times, these sentences comprise two or three full lines of texts. Other times, they take up as many as four lines or even an entire paragraph. This is a problem. Even if these long sentences are not technically run-on or "fused" sentences, it is better to divide them. To clarify this important strategy, consider the following seven examples. Each one begins with an original sentence of two to four lines and continues with an improved version that divides the sentence. An italicized explanation follows each example.

Example #1

Original. From my observations, discussing the setup with the technicians who do work in the room, and in speaking to Taylor Griffin, I am seriously concerned about the short term and long term integrity of our phone room and the equipment in it.

Improved. I am seriously concerned over the short- and long-term integrity of our phone room and its equipment. My concern stems from personal observation and recent discussions with both our technicians and Taylor Griffin.

Note: The writer has good intentions. He sees a serious problem and wants to correct it. The improved version better serves the writer by reversing the content. It foregrounds the police officer's concern and then continues with the source of the concern.

Example #2

Original. Changing to the advocacy center approach is a much better way of doing business both from the standpoint of the prosecutor who is involved in the first phase of the investigation and the victim who is only interviewed two times instead of four or five times.

Improved. The advocacy center approach is a much better way of doing business. Prosecutors involved in the first phase of the investigation will benefit, but victims will too. Instead of being interviewed four or five times, they will be interviewed only twice.

Note: The writer is a hero. He recognizes the current system as inhuman and wants to change it, and the revised sentence will help him accomplish this goal. It features a short "topic sentence" that quickly articulates the writer's belief. The second sentence is the explanation.

Looking Back

Does the final sentence in the improved version of Example #2 need a comma? Which FCA explains the rule?

Looking Back

Does the second-to-the-last sentence in the improved version of Example #2 need a comma? Which FCA explains the rule?

Example #3

Original. This grant was submitted in May of this year with the approval of City Council and the public school system and the original intent was to deploy one officer in the elementary buildings inside the city limits, and the second officer would be deployed at the high school/middle school complex if the school system decided to annex its property into the city.

Improved. This grant was submitted in May of this year with the approval of City Council and the public school system. The original intention, which was based upon annexation plans, was to deploy one officer in the elementary buildings inside the city limits and the second officer at the high school/middle school complex.

Note: The writer is juggling multiple purposes. Most obviously, he is announcing a grant approval, but this announcement also functions as a reminder to renew annexation discussions. The second version better serves the writer. It simply includes a period after "public school system," so that greater emphasis is placed on that approval. In addition, the annexation reference is embedded within the second sentence (instead of tacked on at the end).

Example #4

Original. Our wish is that all motorists be aware of their speed so that we do not have to issue any citations and that all of our children are able to travel to and from school safely.

Improved. We would like all motorists to be more aware of their speed. That way, they won't receive citations and, more importantly, children can safely travel to and from school.

Note: The writer is promoting three related concepts: (1) motorists' awareness of speed, (2) officers' number of citations, and (3) children's safety to/from school. By writing two sentences, the writer emphasizes the cause/effect relationship between these concepts. Note that in the second sentence, "that way" functions as the transition, and "citations" are described from the motorists' viewpoint.

Example #5

Original. I thank you for a job well done, and the particularly professional demeanor that each of you demonstrated when you were faced with this critical situation.

Improved. I thank you for a job well done. In particular, I appreciate the professional demeanor that each of you demonstrated when faced with this critical situation.

Note: The writer has honorable intentions. Though commending more than one person, he clearly wants to emphasize individual effort. To that end, the writer benefits by writing two sentences. The first is a short "topic sentence" that sets purpose. As a separate unit, the second sentence provides greater emphasis to individual professionalism. "In particular" is the transition.

Looking Back

Reread the improved version of Example #5; try to imagine one or two Big Pictures that might have prompted the writer to write. Do you think the writer achieved leadership objectives in writing? Which of the following would apply?

- Build self-image.
- Enhance Public relationships.
- Promote policies and procedures.
- Increase *esprit de corps*.

Example #6

Original. The positions we propose to fill would be seven rifle squad members and one commander position, plus four team members for a color guard team and one commander.

Improved. For the rifle squad and color guard, we propose thirteen positions. They include seven rifle squad members, four color guard members, and two commanders (one for each team).

Note: The writer is proposing thirteen positions. Rather than expecting audience members to add up the numbers, he can highlight the total in the first sentence. The second sentence provides the breakdown.

Looking Back

Reread the improved version of Example #6; there are four numbers in the two sentences: thirteen, seven, four, and two. Why are each of these numbers written as words and not digits? What FCA would clarify this rule?

Example #7

Original. I have been working with Lieutenant Anderson in order to make the transition as smooth as possible and have not run across any major problems other than it is a very time consuming process.

Improved. I have been working with Lieutenant Anderson to make the transition as smooth as possible. So far, I have not run across any major problem, except that the process is time consuming.

Note: The writer is making three points: he has been working with the lieutenant, he has had no major problem, and he finds the transition time consuming. The improved version focuses on the positive. The first sentence is entirely positive, and the second sentence emphasizes the positive because it subordinates "time consuming," which is the only problem. "So far" functions as a transition.

Strategy #2: Eliminating Passive Voice

Police officers are famous for using passive voice, but what exactly is passive voice, and why is it so prevalent in police work? As a starting point in answering these questions, compare two simple sentences: *The child kicked the ball. The ball was kicked.* Of these two sentences, the first is active because the subject of the sentence—the child—"takes" or is doing the action in the sentence (kicking the ball). In contrast, the second sentence is passive because its subject—the ball—is passive. It is not doing anything at all; instead, something is being done to it. Further, it isn't clear who is doing the kicking.

Police officers' tendency to overuse passive voice probably stems from years and years of writing reports. In these reports, investigating officers were traditionally taught or expected to remove themselves as agents to promote an "objective stance," so passive voice became the norm, and it started to "sound right." As clarification, consider these three typical sentences: *It was observed that Mr. Peterson walked across the street. The suspect was advised of his rights and then questioned. The investigation was initiated on December 2.* Despite the use of passive voice in these sentences, a police officer is clearly doing the action. An officer observed Mr. Peterson, an officer advised and questioned the suspect, and an officer initiated an investigation; there is no way around it. However, when any language structure (including passive voice) has been the norm for years, it lingers and even has the power to perpetuate itself from one generation to the next. In other words, old habits—including even sentence structure—are hard to break. Second, passive voice generally takes more words to write than active voice, so it contributes to wordiness that characterizes police documents.

To clarify how to eliminate passive voice, consider the following seven examples. Each one begins with an original sentence in passive voice and continues with the same sentence in active voice. An italicized explanation follows.

Example #1

Passive. The meeting **was led** by CDP Captain Steve Weinstock.

Active. CDP Captain Steve Weinstock **led** the meeting.

Note: The second version is active because the subject (the captain) is doing the action. By using active voice, the writer reduces the word count by over 20%.

Example #2

Passive. A summons will be requested, along with felony charges of theft and falsification, from the county prosecutor.

Active. The county prosecutor will request a summons, along with felony charges of theft and falsification.

Note: The second version is active because the subject (the prosecutor) is doing the action. By using active voice, the writer reduces the word count by 12%.

Example #3

Passive. This form is completed by the lieutenant and reviewed by the chief.

Active. The lieutenant completes this form, and the chief reviews it.

Note: The second version is active because the subjects (the lieutenant and the chief) are doing the action. They are completing or reviewing the form. By using active voice, the writer eliminates word count by nearly 17%.

Looking Back

Why is there a comma in the second sentence? What FCA explains the rule?

Example #4

Passive. Records of the accident are required by insurance companies to process claims made by their clients.

Active. To process their clients' claims, insurance companies require accident records.

Note: The second version is active because the subject of the sentence—insurance companies—is doing the action. They are requiring accident records. By eliminating passive voice, the writer reduces word count by nearly 40%.

Example #5

Passive. Bicycles will be operated in a safe and prudent manner with officer safety as the paramount concern.

Active. Operate bicycles safely and prudently with officer safety as the paramount concern.

Note: The second version is active because the implied subject—you—is doing the action: operating bicycles. By writing in active voice and changing "safe and prudent manner" to "safely and prudently," the writer reduces word count by nearly 30%.

Example #6

Passive. Bicycles are to be stored in the cage on the 5th level of the garage.

Active. Store bicycles in the cage on the 5th level of the garage.

Note: The second version is active because the implied subject—you—is doing the action: storing bicycles in the cage. By writing in active voice, the writer reduces word count by 20%.

Example #7

Passive. The Executive Staff review of the Professional Standards Bureau Inspection of the Division's Evidence Fund has been scheduled for Wednesday, December 19, 2001 during Executive Staff.

Active. At its 12-19-01 meeting, the Executive Staff will review the Professional Standards Bureau Inspection of the Division's Evidence Fund.

Note: The second version is active because the subject of the sentence—the Executive Staff—is doing the action. Its members are reviewing the standards. By writing in active voice and rewording the date, the writer reduces word count by approximately 30%.

Looking Back

Revisit the active version of Example #7 and then explain why its is written without an apostrophe. What FCA explains the rule?

Strategy #3: Reducing Copspeak

Copspeak is a loaded term, and it means different things to different people. It can refer to an entire language system, like a specialized dialect of English, or it can refer to often-used words of phrases, such as "advise" or "tour of duty." For all of these reasons, it is theoretically impossible to provide a comprehensive discussion of copspeak in a single handbook. With this in mind, this section of Chapter Two focuses upon a single aspect of copspeak: strategies for eliminating copspeak that unnecessarily add words.

The following seven examples each begin with a sentence including negative copspeak and then continue with the same sentence without it. An italicized explanation follows.

Example #1

Copspeak. In the event that a report is forwarded to the K-9 Division, please follow these procedures.

Revised: When forwarding reports to the K-9 Division, please follow these procedures.

Note: The phrase, "in the event that," is copspeak. By eliminating it, the writer reduces word count by 37%.

Example #2

Copspeak. I was in attendance at the Laser Shot Shooting Simulation.

Revised.   I attended the Laser Shot Shooting Simulation.

Note: The phrase, "was in attendance," is copspeak. By eliminating it, the writer reduces word count by 30%.

Example #3

Copspeak. Any question or problem is to be directed to Lieutenant Dunbar and/or your turn commander.

Revised.   Direct any question or problem to Lieutenant Dunbar and/or your turn commander.

Note: The phrase, "is to be directed" is copspeak. By rephrasing it, the writer reduces word count by 19%.

Looking Back

Explain the capitalization of the two job titles in Example #3.

Example #4

Copspeak. The BPD has progressed to such a point that the day-to-day operations rely on the use of computers for many of its functions.

Revised.   The BPD relies on computers for most of its daily operations.

Note: This sentence is comprised almost entirely of copspeak. By eliminating it, the writer reduces word count by 56%.

Example #5

Copspeak.   All officers are responsible to comply with policies and procedures, and all supervisors are responsible to address policy and procedure violations when they are observed.

Revised.   All officers are responsible for complying with policies and procedures, and all supervisors are responsible for addressing any violation.

Note: The phrase, "when they are observed," is copspeak. By eliminating it, the writer reduces word count by 28%.

Example #6

Copspeak.   Captain Barl stated that it is in the best interest of all suburbs to work together to plot crime information because the same criminals are committing crimes across jurisdictional borders.

Revised.   According to Captain Barl, criminals work across jurisdictions, and so departments should work together to plot crime information.

Note: This sentence is comprised almost entirely of copspeak. By eliminating it, the writer reduces word count by 40%.

Looking Back

Why are the two commas necessary in the revised sentence?

Looking Back

What Big Picture might have prompted the writer in Example #6 to write in the first place? What leadership initiatives were accomplished in doing so?

- Build self-image.
- Enhance Public relationships.
- Promote policies and procedures.
- Increase *esprit de corps*.

Example #7

Copspeak.   Could you please do a headcount on your respective shift as to the number of officers that need fingerprint kits and training?

Revised.   Could you please indicate how many officers on your shift need fingerprint kits and training?

Note: The phrase, "do a headcount on your respective shift as to the number of officers," is copspeak. By eliminating it, the writer reduces word count by 22%.

Strategy #4: Addressing Repetition and Redundancy

It is understandable why police officers' documents are often times repetitive and redundant. It stems from a desire to be understood. After all, police officers write to a wide range of audience members with different educational backgrounds and experience levels. It is possible, however, to address the needs of a diverse audience in a concise way. The following seven examples illustrate this concept. They are each comprised of an original and revised sentence, followed by an italicized explanation.

Example #1

Wordy.   This is a serious issue, and the chief wants this serious issue corrected immediately

Concise.   This is a serious issue, and the chief wants it corrected immediately.

Note: By eliminating a repeated phrase, the writer reduces word count by 14%.

Looking Back

Do you think "the chief" should be capitalized or not? Why? What does the relevant FCA say about this topic?

Example #2

Wordy.   The Jackson Post currently stands at twelve troopers. One trooper at the Jackson Post is eligible for retirement with an excess of 30 years of service time and three troopers currently have active transfer requests to other posts.

Concise.   The Jackson Post stands at twelve troopers. One trooper is eligible for retirement after 30+ years of service, and three troopers have requested transfers.

Note: This sentence has several examples of words/phrases that are repetitive and/or redundant. By eliminating them, the writer reduces word count by 37%.

Looking Back

Why is the "one" in "One trooper" written as a word, but "30+" in "30+ years of service" isn't? What FCA would explain the rule?

Example #3

Wordy.   Mr. Smith, 4th-Watersted Blockclub, complained of juveniles disturbing the peace, juveniles doing drugs, people urinating in public, and neighbors barbecuing on their porches in the area of West 12th Street and Rowley.

Concise.   Mr. Smith, 4th-Watersted Blockclub, complained of people disturbing the peace, doing drugs, urinating in public and barbecuing on porches in the West 12th Street and Greenway area.

Note: The sentence repeats "juveniles," and the words, "people" and "neighbors" are synonymous. By eliminating and/or combining, the writer reduces word count by 15%.

Example #4

Wordy.   The use of dogs in police work has changed from the 1960's when dogs were used as crowd control and guard duty.

Concise.   K-9 units have changed since the 1960s. Police departments no longer use them for crowd control or guard duty.

Note: The phrase, "the use of," is redundant, and "dogs" is repetitive. By eliminating both, the writer reduces word count by 17%.

Example #5

Wordy.   To gather emergency phone number listings from business owners in the community to aid our agency if the need to contact them in an emergency arises.

Concise.   To gather community business owners' emergency phone numbers.

Note: The first sentence repeats "emergency" and unnecessarily includes the phrases, "listings from" and "in the community." By eliminating them, the writer reduces word count by 70%.

Example #6

Wordy.   Sam was an impressive police applicant, as I remember it.

Concise.   Sam was an impressive police applicant.

Note: The phrase, "as I remember it," is redundant. By eliminating it, the writer reduces word count by 40%.

Example #7

Wordy.   The content was good, but in my case about one half of it was repetitive as I had had the class about twelve years ago.

Concise.   The course was good, but I had taken it in 1990, so about half the content was repetitive.

Note: The phrases, "in my case," and "as I had had the class about twelve years ago" are repetitive and redundant. By eliminating them, the writer reduces word count by 28%.

Strategy #5: Cutting Words "Here & There"

Cutting words "here and there" is reminiscent of a backpacking adage: *To reduce pounds, pay attention to ounces*. The same holds true in written communication for police officers. To write sentences that really are "clear, concise, and to the point," pay attention to random unnecessary words. The following examples are designed to illustrate this concept. Each example is, again, comprised of an original and revised version of the same sentence. An italicized explanation follows.

Example #1

Wordy. The purpose of this program is to assist officers in meeting their personal goals while meeting the needs of the community.

Concise. The program purpose is to help officers simultaneously meet personal goals and community needs.

Note: By cutting words "here and there," the writer reduces word count by 33%.

Looking Back

Revisit FCA #3 and then explain why the noun/pronoun combination, "officers /their personal goals" is correct.

Example #2

Wordy. Mr. Albertson sent a letter of complaint and alleges that Officer Tomlinson made unprofessional comments.

Concise. Mr. Albertson's complaint letter alleges that Officer Tomlinson made unprofessional comments.

Note: By cutting words "here and there," the writer reduces word count by27%.

Example #3

Wordy. The thought of talking to your children about the dangers of today's society can seem scary.

Concise.   Talking to your children about society's dangers can seem scary.

Note: By cutting words "here and there," the writer reduces word count by 31%.

Looking Back

Try to imagine four different Big Pictures that might have prompted the writer in Example #3 to write. Given the four different sets of circumstances, what other information might have been included in the document?

Example #4

Wordy.   In addition, the equipment purchased for the lab will have other applications within the department.

Concise.   In addition, the proposed lab equipment will have other departmental applications.

Note: By cutting words "here and there," the writer reduces word count by27%.

Example #5

Wordy.   To assist all employees in preparing themselves for accepting positions of greater responsibility.

Concise.   To help prepare employees for accepting positions of greater responsibility.

Note: By cutting words "here and there," the writer reduces word count by23%.

Example #6

Wordy.   The course needed to train additional officers in the future is available through OPOTA and is only a two-day course.

Concise.   OPOTA offers a two-day training course for officers.

Note: By cutting words "here and there," the writer reduces word count by 57%.

Example #7

Wordy.   In addition, there are to be no "creative" uniform adjustments.

Concise.   In addition, policy prohibits "creative" uniform adjustments.

Note: By cutting words "here and there," the writer reduces word count by30%.

Chapter Review

Most police officers claim they value writing that is "clear, concise, and to the point," but their own individual sentences suggest the opposite. In fact, most police officers would benefit by learning to write sentences more concisely.

Five strategies for writing more concisely are (1) dividing long sentences, (2) eliminating passive voice, (3) reducing copspeak, (4) addressing repetition and redundancy, and (5) cutting words "here and there." By following these strategies, police officers could reduce word count by as much as 25% or even 30%.

For Discussion

1. In classroom settings, students sometimes try to make their writing as long as possible to follow teachers' page length guidelines; using large print font and/or wide margins are two good examples. It is also possible, however, to make papers longer by writing wordy sentences. Do you remember classmates doing this, or did you do it, yourself? If yes, what strategies did you or your peers use to add unnecessary words?
2. Define copspeak. Write five sentences that make you "sound like a cop." Circle the words or phrases in the sentences that represent copspeak.
3. Why do you think that police documents are often so wordy?
4. How would you explain the difference between active and passive voice? Can you think of a good reason a police officer might want to use passive voice?
5. Write a thirty-word sentence on a topic of your choice; then condense the word count by 10%, 20%, and even 30%. What strategies did you use?
6. Assuming the overall messages are identical in content, would you rather read a short or longer letter or directive?

Test Yourself

Practice Exercises #3.1

Here are ten sentences taken directly from actual police documents. Read them carefully to identify (a) the police officer's message and (b) the crucial content. Then, using any or all of the five strategies from this chapter, rewrite the sentences so that they really are "clear, concise, and to the point."

1. My last suggestion would be to add school closings and delays to the Website for fast review as opposed to a crawl across the television screen or listening for the school closings on the radio.

2. Some victims have been advised to call us back if the damage to their property was permanent or to just "exchange insurance information," only to have them later needing a report before their insurance will cover damage.

3. Because the shift was already scheduled at the minimum limit of nine officers and now only one dispatcher who was already on overtime, an officer had to be called in on overtime to maintain safety levels.

4. Although it is ultimately your responsibility to ensure that your actions do not conflict with any policy or practice currently in use, completing the course evaluation form in a detailed manner helps catch conflicting issues and minimize the change of conflicts later.

5. This communication is being forwarded to you as a conclusion of fact report upon conclusion of the internal complain you filed with this department on April 11.

6. "Critical Incident" is defined as any natural disaster, biological, nuclear, incendiary, chemical or explosive situation, or civil disturbance of such magnitude that it requires the development of a command post and the calling out of additional officers or specialized units of the local police department or other public services.

7. My confusion comes from what is to be determined to be a "noise complaint," since many calls we respond to could be interpreted as a "noise complaint," even though the intent of the call has nothing to do with noise.

8. During previous events, the Fire Department expressed concerns with the difficult in maneuvering their equipment around the corners of Sudlet Drive and requested that we restrict parking on the interior portions of the curves to address this problem.

9. If you already are certified, you do not have to attend, but are encouraged to, to remain proficient in the tactical baton.

10. Though the originally proposed schedule consisted of only one permanent shift, it has come to my attention that a derivative of this schedule has been proposed which would call for one permanent dayshift squad as well, while the remaining two squads would rotate on the thirty-two day rotation.

Practice Set #3.2

Here are ten sentences taken directly from actual police documents. Read them carefully to identify (a) the police officer's message and (b) the crucial content. Then, using any or all of the five strategies from this chapter, rewrite the sentences so that they really are "clear, concise, and to the point."

1. Although you may wish to have me consult Internet security or records management before the idea can for much further, I would appreciate your initial thoughts on the matter to this point.

2. When driving, officers should be wearing their seatbelts (Why not? We're ticking the public for it!), as well as obeying all other traffic laws (using turn signals, following the speed limit during regular operations, coming to a complete stop at stop signs, and not disobeying do-not-enter signs).

3. Concerned for your safety, the officers asked you to move your vehicle because it was not safe for you to sit on the shoulder of the road and suggested you pull off just up the road in a parking lot where it would be safer.

4. Officers were instructed that it is their responsibility to check the oil, windshield wiper fluid and gasoline, noting any deficiencies on the inspection form and advised the watch supervisor to assure that the problem can be corrected.

5. In the discussion about having an electronic interactive type of newsletter or bulletin board, you had mentioned that email and/or other electronic documents are treated like hard copy documents generated within the department in terms of their being public record.

6. It was determined that the awards may be presented in groupings by type of award.

7. In investigating and compiling information on the above stated personnel, it was found the candidate exhibited extreme desire to become a part of this organization, not in just to "powers that be" to get the appointment, but the general public in her day-to-day contacts.

8. From his initial response and assessment of the situation to his ongoing follow-up with the family even several days after the incident occurred, Patrol Officer Jamison is to be commended for his tact, courtesy, and professionalism.

9. I gave her a business card and asked for her information and she refused to give it to me and she again stated that she was going to file a complaint on me and I advised her that the chief was on his way to take her complain and she stated that was a good thing.

10. Once it is determined that the child meets the above listed criteria, the turn commander shall go to the scene and insure that the necessary incident reports, as well as the Amber Alert Forms from the Sheriff's Office are completed (All turn commanders have been supplied with the necessary forms).

Practice Set #3.3

Here are ten sentences taken directly from actual police documents. Read them carefully to identify (a) the police officer's message and (b) the crucial content. Then, using any or all of the five strategies from this chapter, rewrite the sentences so that they really are "clear, concise, and to the point."

1. It was suggested to me by Patrol Officer McTavet that we check with public school officials and try to get a cooperative effort in dealing the high school students that commit traffic offenses going to and from school.

2. I would like to take this opportunity to congratulate and commend you on the obvious and apparent hard work and effort that you have personally done concerning the recent police promotional procedure.

3. The submission of confirmation of attendance forms after your training courses has been intermittent.

4. On August 13, Police Specialist Michael Taggart and his police canine partner were assigned to the Robbery Task Force and were patrolling in the area of the 1200 block on Waverly Road in District Eight.

5. I see no issue with the time the correction officers used to secure the subject and his belongs prior to granting his request, especially since he was combative with officers and had fought them during his arrest.

6. If the concerns are non-suspicious, such as the mail was unexpected During my conversation with Captain Albertson, I thought I told him to get me a memo and I would look into resolving the problem.

7. This was done since there have been discussions that the system would be used by the County Sheriff's Office and, therefore, they would share in a portion of the system's costs, as well.

8. If the drugs need to go to the lab for analysis, we don't want to have to send the entire container or damage the sealed container by having to op it to remove the drugs for analysis.

9. While there are no full proof strategies to prevent identify theft from taking place, some of the above mentioned measures may protect you and everything you have worked so hard to earn.

10. I began my inquiry into the background check of Donald Ambersand for his consideration as an applicant for the position of dispatcher here with the APD.

Practice Set #3.4

Here are ten sentences taken directly from actual police documents. Read them carefully to identify (a) the police officer's message and (b) the crucial content. Then, using any or all of the five strategies from this chapter, rewrite the sentences so that they really are "clear, concise, and to the point."

1. The primary issue of the appeal dealt with a memo that was distributed by ODH concerning breath testing, which stated that an "invalid sample" reading should initiate another twenty-minute observation period.

2. The second option which this office would more readily find compliant to true policy is that Cadet McCall consider either a leave of absence pending enrollment in a police academy or resignation pending reappointment following completion of police academy.

3. Once all information is obtained and confirmed by the investigating officer it will be turned over to the dispatcher.

4. I believe that this request for training will be beneficial to Officer Mowers and the unit, as his investigations are now administrative/internal that involve employee rights, as opposed to criminal and employment issues.
5. Once it has been determined a suspect may meet the protocol of the program, the information should be forwarded to ATF who would then take the case through the federal system.

MyCompLab—Optional Exercises and Activities

As the homepage shows, MyCompLab is divided into three sections: Grammar, Writing, and Research.

Under Grammar, complete exercises/activities from the following sections:

- Click ExerciseZone and then select the following: Parallel Structure, Redundancy and Wordiness, and Stringy Sentences (found under Usage and Style), as well as Voice – Active/Passive (found under Sentence Editing).
- Click Grammar Video Tutorials and then select/watch Lack of Parallel Structure and Wordiness/Redundancy (both found under Top 20 Grammar Errors).

Under Writing, complete exercises/activities from the following sections:

- Click Writing Process Exercises and then select Clarifying Sentences (found under Revising) and Improving Sentence Flow (under Finishing).
- Click Model Documents and select one or two academic or nonacademic documents identified by your instructor. Analyze these documents for concise sentence structure, circling any wordy sentences that you find. Last, provide a more concise revision of each circled sentence and be prepared to share them with classmates.

CHAPTER FOUR

MONITORING PARAGRAPH LENGTH

I hope my written communication reinforces my credibility as a thoughtful, fair, and articulate leader.

Sergeant Michael J. Eagan
Huber Heights Police Division
Huber Heights, Ohio

Leadership Objectives

- To learn to monitor paragraph length; to see leadership value in doing so.
- To recognize that good paragraph length enhances visual impact and reading comprehension.
- To recognize a basic paragraph structure: topic sentence followed by supporting information.
- To understand three general rules for monitoring paragraph length: (1) write short introductions and conclusions, (2) avoid documents comprised of one overly long paragraph, (3) avoid documents comprised of a series of very short paragraphs.

Assess Yourself

Ask yourself the following questions:

- What is a paragraph?
- Have you been taught that paragraphs should be a specific number of sentences? If yes, how many?
- How long or short do your paragraphs tend to be?
- Can you define topic sentence? What is supporting information?
- How do paragraph boundaries relate to visual impact and, in turn, the writer's professional image and audience members' reading comprehension?

Appropriate paragraph length is linked to the Power of the Pen. When police officers write paragraphs that are consistently too long or too short, they compromise visual impact because their documents look unprofessional and poorly organized, which, in turn, reflects negatively on the police officer and his/her police department. Equally important, inappropriate paragraph length may also compromise reading comprehension and, in turn, leadership initiatives and departmental productivity. An important feature of any good police document, then, is appropriate paragraph length.

Despite claims to the contrary, no "perfect length" or "specific number of sentences" exists when it comes to writing paragraphs. Instead, it's more productive to consider basic paragraph structure. What exactly is a paragraph? What purpose does it serve? A paragraph is often described as a unit, a unit of several sentences organized around a specific topic. The first sentence in most paragraphs, but especially in professional communication, is traditionally a topic sentence. As its label suggests, the *topic sentence* alerts readers to *the topic* at hand, and it provides unity and direction for the remaining, or supporting, sentences in the paragraph.

To clarify paragraph structure, consider the sample paragraphs excerpted from two separate documents. The first is a paragraph from a counseling document written by Sergeant Wendy Loomis of the Lake County Sheriff's Office (Writing Sample 4.1), and the second is a revised version of a memo written by an anonymous sergeant from a police department in Ohio (Writing Sample 4.2).

Writing Sample 4.1

As I discussed with you, a thirty-minute personal phone call is not acceptable because we all must work together as a team. When one dispatcher is busy on the phone or radio, the others have to be cognizant and able to assist in answering their designated lines. Though you did not miss any radio/phone lines on your desk during the personal phone call, the other dispatchers were taking several calls and placing others on hold, along with answering the radios. Equally important, you must remember that all calls are recorded and can be requested by the public or media at any time. If this request takes place in your case, it would be very embarrassing not only for you, but also for the entire department.

Looking Back

The previous message is a negative message; however, how do you believe the recipient responded? Is it possible or even probable that this message helped to build *esprit de corps*? Why?

Writing Sample 4.2

The new system calls for two procedural changes. First, each detective has been assigned a file drawer for all his/her open cases. This file draw should continuously house all relevant working materials for each open case (take home no originals!). The need for this file drawer system is clear; it provides immediate access of all open cases to supervisors from other shifts, in case (a) a victim calls for an update or (b) a development occurs. Second, each detective will meet with me on a monthly basis to review all open cases. My goal here is not related to performance evaluation. Instead, my purpose is to gain a better understanding of each open case in order to provide any guidance or support.

> ### Looking Back
>
> Reread the first sentence in the previous paragraph: *The new system calls for two procedural changes.* Why did the sergeant write the number "two" as a word and not a digit?

Compare the overall structure of the two sample paragraphs. Notice that Sergeant Loomis' first sentence is a topic sentence for the paragraph because it sets the purpose—the importance of working as a team—and it is then followed by a series of sentences that clarify and support that claim. The same is true for the anonymous sergeant's paragraph. It begins with a topic sentence introducing the two procedural changes, so readers know what to expect. The following sentences support the topic sentence by either identifying a procedural change or explaining it. Note: Topic sentences aren't always the first sentence in a paragraph; however, they often are in professional communication.

Three Basic Rules for Monitoring Paragraph Length

As the sample paragraphs show, basic paragraph structure is typically comprised of two parts: a topic sentence and supporting sentences. Though paragraph variations exist (just analyze any novel, newspaper column, or essay), this combination of topic sentence and supporting sentences provides unity to the paragraph and direction for the reader. In addition to understanding this basic structure, however, police officers can also monitor paragraph length by understanding three general paragraphing rules that apply especially to police documents.

Paragraph Rule #1 – Write Short Introductions/Conclusions

Introductions and conclusions are often short paragraphs. In fact, it's appropriate that either one or both be comprised of just one or two sentences.

As Chapter Seven explains, the introduction often articulates the writer's purpose, and it is general practice to conclude with a closing sentence or two.

Writing Sample 4.3 and 4.4 showcase, respectively, five introductions and conclusions, each comprised appropriately of one to three sentences.

Writing Sample 4.3

On April 6, I was dispatched to 41 Main Street about a "loud music" complaint.

The APD announces the Citizen's Police Academy to begin on September 24.

I'm writing to commend Officers Stewart and Gleason for outstanding job performance on August 23. As the following narrative shows, their work resulted in the successful resolution of a dangerous and volatile situation.

Please accept this application to attend the Police Executive Leadership College (PELC) for the upcoming session.

Effective April 1, the PPD will park cars at Breven Parking Lot located on Fender Avenue. This change stems from the rising cost of courthouse parking and a cost comparison of parking garages. To make the transition as smooth as possible, please follow these directions:

Looking Back

Reconsider the five introductions in Writing Sample 4.3. What do you suppose is the Big Picture for each introduction?

Writing Sample 4.4

If you have questions, please see your shift supervisor ASAP.

Thank you for your consideration.

Please let me know if I may be of further assistance. My phone number is . . .

I would welcome the opportunity to discuss this proposal in person. Perhaps we could meet after the City Council meeting next week.

I will follow up this letter with a telephone call next week. Thank you!

Looking Back

Reread this sentence: *Please let me know if I may be of further assistance.* Explain why the writer selected "may be" (instead of "maybe") and "further (instead of "farther").

Looking Back

Reread these two sentences:

- *If you have questions, please see your shift supervisor ASAP.*
- *Perhaps we could meet after the City Council meeting next week.*

First, why is "shift supervisor" not capitalized and "City Council" is?

Second, What does ASAP stand for? Is this an acceptable abbreviation? Why or why not?

Paragraph Rule #2 – Avoid Documents Comprised of One Long Paragraph

Creating a document comprised of one long paragraph is a common paragraphing mistake in the field of law enforcement. It is an approach that compromises visual impact and, in turn, the police officer's professional self-image. In addition, readers may actually "lose their way" while reading, depending on the paragraph length. One overly long paragraph, however, is easily corrected by simply dividing it into two or three separate paragraphs. To clarify, consider the following document pairs written by Sergeant Wendy Loomis of the Lake County Sheriff's Office (Writing Sample 4.5A & B) and Sergeant John Mason of the Heath Police Department (Writing Sample 4.6A & B):

Looking Back

As you read Writing Sample 4.5A & B, please describe what appears to be the Big Picture. What is the purpose and audience? What prompted the writer to write? Speculate about the writer's planning, drafting, revision, and polishing strategies.

Looking Back

As you read Writing Sample 4.5B, notice that both the introduction and conclusion are very short (but effective) paragraphs.

Writing Sample 4.5A
Original Version

DATE

TO: All Units
FR: Sergeant Wendy Loomis
RE: The 911 Transfer Box

We have a new piece of equipment in dispatch. It is a 911 transfer box, which in an emergency, by flipping a switch, will roll our 911 calls to Mentor PD. This box is located by the sirens—white in color—and has the word, "informer," in the upper left-hand corner. Should we have to evacuate the building, Mentor PD can be notified via radio and someone will have to turn the switch on. In order to switch the toggle, you must lift up on the toggle and then press it upward. That's it! It also has an alarm and a mute bottom; I do not know of a reason why it would alarm; however, press the mute bottom if it happens and notify any OIC. If you have any question, please see your shift sergeant.

Writing Sample 4.5B
Revised Version

DATE

TO: All Units
FR: Sergeant Wendy Loomis
RE: The 911 Transfer Box

We have a new piece of dispatch equipment: a 911 transfer. In an emergency, it will roll all of our 911 calls to the Mentor Police Department.

The transfer box is easy to operate. It's located by the sirens, is white in color, and has the word, "informer," in the upper left-hand corner. Should we have an emergency evacuation or major phone line problem, the Mentor PD can be notified via radio and then a dispatcher simply needs to flip a switch. This is easily accomplished by lifting on the toggle and then pressing it upward. That's it! The transfer box also has an alarm and a mute bottom. It's not clear why the box would alarm; however, if it happens, simply press the mute button and notify any OIC.

If you have questions about this new equipment, please see your shift supervisor.

The original and revised versions of Sergeant Loomis's memo serve the same excellent leadership purpose: to introduce the 911 transfer equipment. It's crucial that the entire police department understand what this equipment is and how to operate it. Though Writing Sample 4.5A includes all of the necessary information, Writing Sample 4.5B better serves Sergeant Loomis. First, it looks more professional on the page, so her professional self-image is also enhanced. Equally important, readers are more likely to read and understand her message. The first paragraph sets the purpose, the second paragraph describes how easy the 911 transfer is to find and use, and the conclusion is a standard close. Monitoring paragraph length makes a big difference.

Now consider Sergeant Mason's memo:

Writing Sample 4.6A
Original Version

DATE

TO: Sergeant Scott Snow
FR: Sergeant John Mason
RE: Response to Active Shootings Training

I wanted to thank you for providing our officers with the opportunity to train side by side with yours. For a small department, like ours, it is imperative to make efficient use of the mutual aide agreement. The chance to duplicate tactics by training together for this response was most beneficial. I hope in the future we can coordinate more training, or maybe develop a countywide protocol for these incidents. Our officers had many praises for the sessions and gave high marks to the instructors. Captain Stollard did a fine job of relating the urgency and importance of the subject to those in attendance. And of course you and Sergeant Haren did a fine job of organizing the entire operation. Thanks again and please contact me if there is anything that HPD can do for you.

Writing Sample 4.6B
Revised Version

DATE

TO: Sergeant Scott Snow, Training Office
FR: Sergeant John Mason, Training Sergeant
RE: Response to Active Shootings Training

I wanted to thank you for providing our officers with the opportunity to train side by side with yours. For a small department, like ours, it is imperative to make efficient use of the mutual aide agreement. Our officers had many praises for the sessions and gave high marks to the instructors. Captain Stollard did a fine job of relating the urgency and importance of the subject to those in attendance. And of course you and Sergeant Haren did a find job of organizing the entire operation.

Thanks again! Please contact me if there is anything that HPD can do for you. I hope in the future we can coordinate more training or maybe develop a countywide protocol for these incidents.

Looking Back

What prompted Sergeant Mason to write this memo? In other words, what was the Big Picture? Would a phone call have achieved the same leadership purpose as a letter? Why? What other leadership initiatives may have resulted from writing?

The original and revised versions of Sergeant Mason's memo are both thank-you letters, written in response to a mutually beneficial training opportunity between departments. In writing, Sergeant Mason does more than express thanks; he also promotes good PR for himself and his department. Even so, Writing Sample 4.6B is stronger because of monitored paragraph length. Instead of one large paragraph in the original document, a two-paragraph format looks more professional and is more logical too. The first paragraph expresses thanks and documents the side-by-side training that took place, and the second paragraph is a standard conclusion, with one variation: Sergeant Mason's hope that the two departments can work together in future training endeavors.

Paragraph Rule #3 – Avoid a Series of Very Short Paragraphs

One of the more common paragraphing mistakes is writing documents comprised of a series of very short paragraphs. This approach ruins visual impact, undermining the writer's professional image and credibility, but the resolution is simple: combine paragraphs with related content. To clarify, consider the document pairs written by Lieutenant Chris Elliott of the University of Cincinnati Police Department (4.7A & B) and Sergeant Mikel Carter of the Mason Police Department (4.8A & B).

Writing Sample 4.7A
Original Version

On May 3, I verbally counseled Officer Patrick Wojak regarding sleeping on duty. He stated that it wouldn't happen again. On 8/5/03, two witnesses saw Officer Wojak sleeping in Room G51A of the University Hospital. On 8/13/03, he was seen sleeping in the squad room next to the computer workstation.

Sleeping on duty constitutes a violation of the University of Cincinnati's Policies and Procedures Manual for Conduct: 15-02 Section 2r (Sleeping on the Job) and 15-02 section 2j (Neglect of Duty).

The conduct also violates UPCPD Rules and Regulations section 550.0311 (Sleeping on Duty) and 550.0310 (Neglect of Duty).

Future violations will result in disciplinary actions up to and including termination.

Writing Sample 4.7B
Revised Version

On 5/03/03, Officer Patrick Wojak was verbally counseled by me regarding sleeping on duty, and he stated that it wouldn't happen again. Since then, however, Officer Wojak has been seen sleeping on two separate occasions. On 8/5/03, two witnesses saw him sleeping in Room G51A of the University Hospital. On 8/13/03, Officer Blackwell was also seen sleeping in the squad room next to the computer workstation.

Sleeping on duty violates four different departmental mandates. First, it constitutes a violation of the University of Cincinnati's Policies and Procedures Manual for Conduct: 15-02 Section 2r (Sleeping on the Job) and 15-02 section 2j (Neglect of Duty). Second, the conduct violates UPCPD Rules and Regulations section 550.0311 (Sleeping on Duty) and 550.0310 (Neglect of Duty).

Future violations will result in additional disciplinary actions up to and including termination.

In Writing Sample 4.7A & B, Lieutenant Elliott is writing with the best of leadership intentions because he is obliged to document the officer's negligent behavior. As the two versions of his memo show, the officer in question has been caught sleeping at work on three separate times, which is a violation of four different departmental policies. He needs a reprimand, and the written word is clearly the most effective and far reaching approach. Though both versions provide the same basic information, the revised version is more effective for two reasons. First, the initial paragraph includes a transition sentence: *Since then, Officer Wojak has been seen sleeping on two separate occasions.* In addition to serving as a transition between the first and third sentence, though, this sentence emphasizes the seriousness of the officer's offence because Lieutenant Elliott is doing more than simply stating the facts; he is interpreting them for readers. Second, Officer Elliott combines all of the violations into a single paragraph in the second version and then adds an effective topic sentence: *Sleeping on duty violates four different departmental mandates*. Though the four violations come from two separate documents, it is logical to list all four in the same paragraph.

Now consider Sergeant Carter's memo.

Writing Sample 4.8A
Original Version

I am in the process of asking for financial assistance from the Warren County Commissioners for the Warren County Tactical Response Unit.

Chief Ferrell directed me to also forward our "wish list" to you for possible homeland security funding. Please find this list attached.

If you have any questions, please call me at the Mason Police Department or email me at mcarter@masonoh.org.

Writing Sample 4.8B
Revised Version

Chief Ferrell asked me to write to you regarding the two attached documents. As you can see, the first document is a proposal for financial assistance from the Warren County Commissioners for the Tactical Response Unit. It should arrive at the County Commissioner's office within the next week. The second document is a departmental "wish list" for possible homeland security funding.

If you have questions, please call me at the Mason Police Department or email me at mcarter@masonoh.org.

Looking Back

Reconsider Writing Samples 4.5A, 4.6A, 4.7A, and 4.8A in light of Writing as a Process. A good drafting strategy is to get down ideas, without regard for format, including paragraph length. This means a first draft could easily be comprised of a single paragraph, but a necessary revision activity would to divide the single paragraph.

The original version of Sergeant Carter's memo (Writing Sample 4.8 A) is a series of three paragraphs, each one merely one or two sentences long. Though his leadership intentions are clear and strong, the document lacks good visual impact, and so Sergeant Carter's credibility is potentially compromised. In contrast, the paragraph boundaries in the revised version (Writing Sample 4.8 B) make more sense. The document begins by invoking Chief Ferrell and then directing readers' attention immediately to the two attached documents: the Tactical Response Unit proposal and the Mason Police Department wish list. The revised paragraph structure enhances visual impact, provides a more professional image for the writer, and it is more likely to catch readers' attention from the start.

Chapter Review

Appropriate paragraph length enhances visual impact and, in turn, the professional image of both the police officer and his/her police department. In addition, it enhances reading comprehension, so leadership goals are more likely to be understood and initiated.

A paragraph is a unit of sentences generally comprised of a topic sentence (which identifies the topic of the paragraph) and supporting sentences (which support the topic sentence). Despite claims to the contrary, there is no single or "perfect" number of sentences that constitute a paragraph.

Three basic paragraphing rules apply to law enforcement documents: (1) write very short introductions/conclusions, (2) Avoid writing documents comprised of a single, overly long paragraph, (3) Avoid writing documents comprised of a series of very short paragraphs.

For Discussion

1. What is a paragraph?
2. Why does it make sense for the introduction and conclusion to be very short paragraphs?
3. Why shouldn't documents be comprised of one long paragraph or several very short paragraphs? What is the best way to resolve either paragraphing flaw?
4. Paragraph conventions differ from one field to the next and from genre to genre. Collect a range of ten different types of documents—everything from a newspaper column to a scholarly article—and analyze differences in paragraph length, as well as topic sentence and overall organization. What are the differences and why do you think they exist?
5. In double spaced documents, new paragraphs must begin with an indented first line, but in single spaced documents, indention is not required; instead, double spacing between paragraphs is. Why do you suppose this convention is true?
6. How is good paragraph length connected to visual impact and, in turn, leadership?

Test Yourself

Practice Set #4.1

Compare the two versions of the memo written by Lieutenant Jeff Braley of the Hamilton Township Police Department and then answer the questions following them.

Original Version

DATE
TO: Frank Richardson, Chief
FR: Jeff Braley, Lieutenant
RE: Commendation for Officer Roger Gilbert

It is my request that you would accept this letter as a letter of commendation for Officer Roger Gilbert. Over the past twelve months, Officer Gilbert through his diligent patrol work has taken a large amount of narcotics, namely marijuana, off of the streets of Hamilton Township. The effects of this effort have helped CID learn contacts, as well as dealers, to aid us in our investigations.

Officer Gilbert's actions are greatly appreciated and should serve as an example of what a patrol can accomplish in our township. His actions have led to a number of arrests, as well as a seized vehicle now being used by our division. My only regret is that I did not write this letter sooner.

Once again, if you would have any questions regarding this, I would be happy to discuss them with you at your earliest convenience.

Revised Version

DATE
TO: Frank Richardson, Chief
FR: Jeff Braley, Lieutenant
RE: Commendation for Officer Roger Gilbert

Please accept this memo as a commendation for Officer Roger Gilbert. Through his diligent patrol work over the past twelve months, Officer Gilbert has taken a large amount of narcotics, namely marijuana, off of the streets of Hamilton Township. His efforts have helped CID learn contacts, as well as dealers, to aid us in our investigations. As a result, his actions have led to a number of drug-related arrests, as well as a seized vehicle, which is now being used by our division. Officer Gilbert's actions are greatly appreciated and should serve as an example of what a patrol can accomplish in our township. My only regret is that I did not write this letter sooner.

If you have questions regarding this commendation, I would be happy to discuss them with you at your earliest convenience.

Questions

1. What is the Big Picture of this document? What is the writer's leadership purpose?
2. What is the difference in paragraph structure in the two versions? Which version has better visual impact?
3. How do both versions demonstrate that the writer is an excellent police officer?

Practice Set #4.2

Read the commendation written by Chief Gregory Loftus of the Cleveland Metroparks Ranger Department and then answer the questions that follow it.

DATE
Captain Daniel J. Veloski
Cleveland Metroparks Ranger Headquarters
Fairview Park, Ohio

Dear Captain Veloski:

On behalf of the Metroparks Ranger Department, I would like to thank you for the outstanding job you did in developing and training Cleveland Metroparks personnel in emergency management. You tirelessly coordinated this project with Park Operations, the Law Department, and with outside counsel. I received numerous compliments from Cleveland Metroparks staff who attended your presentations, along with the attached Significant Incident Report from Dr. Robert Hinkle.

I recognize your valuable contribution, not only in actions of this nature, but in the everyday attitude and attention you provide to this agency. Your leadership-by-example style continues to present a stellar model of effective supervisory practice that is elevating the attitude and service of not only those under your direct command, but Cleveland Metroparks Ranger Department as a whole. Your professionalism, dedication, and spirit of cooperation help us to achieve our mission.

Sincerely,

Gregory M. Loftus
Chief

Questions

1. What is the Big Picture of this document? What is writer's leadership intentions? Why do you think he "copied" Captain Veloski's personnel file?
2. What is the purpose of the first paragraph, and how does it differ from the purpose of the second paragraph? Why does the second paragraph strengthen in the letter?
3. Here is the Cleveland Metroparks Ranger Department mission statement: *Providing superior service and law enforcement through proactive, innovative, and unbiased practices.* Based upon the letter, do you think that Captain Veloski wants to achieve the departmental mission?
4. Would you recommend revising this commendation in any manner?

Practice Set #4.3

Read this report written by Sergeant David Gehringer of the Lebanon Police Department and then answer the questions following it.

DATE

TO: Pat Clements, Ken Burns, Bob Hawley, Rick Bens

FR: David Gehringer

RE: Sobriety Checkpoint

On November 19, the Lebanon Police Department conducted a sobriety checkpoint, as planned, on SR 42 near Silverwood Farms. The checkpoint was announced in various media forms and was conducted with seven officers. The purpose of the checkpoint was to create a deterrent to those who would drive impaired within the City of Lebanon.

The checkpoint started at 8:30 PM and lasted until midnight. Over two hundred vehicles were stopped during the checkpoint. Interviewing officers advise that the response of the drivers was overwhelmingly positive and supportive of our actions.

As a direct result of the checkpoint, four drivers were tested for intoxication. Of those four drivers, one was arrested for driving while intoxicated. In addition, two arrests were made in relation to drug offenses, three seatbelt citations were issued, and several warnings were given for administrative offenses.

A debriefing was held immediately after the checkpoint was finished. Information was developed about the mechanism of a sobriety checkpoint. All officers agreed that the mission of the checkpoint was fulfilled, and they discussed improvement ideas for additional sobriety checkpoints.

Overall, the sobriety checkpoint must be considered a great success as part of an ongoing program to deter impaired driving. Patrol Officer Wetzel performed well as the checkpoint supervisor. Additionally, the success could not have been achieved without help from other city departments. Dan Wilson and the Streets Department did a fantastic job manufacturing the signs necessary for the checkpoint, and they delivered the signs, as well as other traffic control items, to us. Thanks to Chief Hannigan and the Fire Department for delivery of lights and a generator. And last, I offer appreciation to Jim Baldwin and Telecom for advertising the checkpoint on Channel Six.

Questions

1. What is the Big Picture of this report? What are the writer's leadership intentions?
2. What other administrative documents might a sobriety checkpoint prompt?
3. How could the report be even stronger? Revise it for improved paragraph length.
4. Would you recommend revising this document in any other manner?

MyCompLab—Optional Exercises and Activities

As the homepage shows, MyCompLab is divided into three sections: Grammar, Writing, and Research.

Under Grammar, complete exercises/activities from the following sections:

- Click ExerciseZone and select Transitional Expressions (found under Sentence Grammar). Complete the Basic/Intermediate Exercises and then consider how a better understanding of transitional phrases and coherence will enhance paragraph development. Next, complete the Intermediate/Advanced Exercises, which focus specifically upon paragraph development.
- Click Grammar Video and select Ineffective or Missing Transition between Paragraphs. Watch this video and then write a letter to your instructor summarizing the content of the video and its useful to you.

Under Writing, complete exercises/activities from the following sections:

- Click Writing Process Exercises and then select Writing Body Paragraphs and Working with Transitions (both found under Drafting), as well as Sharpening Your Paragraphs (found under Revising). Complete these exercises, as your instructor requests.
- Click Writing Video Tutorials and then select/watch Achieving Paragraph Unity (found under Writing in Action Series). How does the information in the video support, enhance, or extend your understanding of paragraph development. How is the information relevant to police officers?

- Click Model Documents and select a document or two identified by your instructor. Analyze this document(s) for well developed paragraphs. Is there a topic sentence; if yes, where is it located? Are remaining paragraphs developed and persuasive? Why or why not? Be prepared to share your work with classmates.

PART TWO

EFFECTIVE POLICE REPORTS: LEADING BY EXAMPLE

The police report is the most commonly written document in any police department. It doesn't matter whether the police department is located in urban, suburban, or rural settings, or whether police officers' tours take place in police departments, sheriff's offices, highway patrols, or college campuses. Everyone writes reports. Typically, the first on-the-job document that cadets and new officers write is a report, but veteran and ranked officers are just as likely to be found writing, or at least evaluating, them.

The police report, however, is arguably even more than the most commonly written document. According to Michael Robinson, the former Director of the Michigan Department of State Police, it is THE leadership foundation of any good police department. In the Introduction to the *Report Writing Handbook*, Robinson claims the following:

> Successful, thorough investigations are some of the keys that help create professional police agencies. In the eyes of the public, today's law enforcement officer is not only charged with protecting citizens, but solving crimes in an efficient and timely manner. In order to fulfill the latter point, an officer must be able to place facts, thoughts, and ideas on paper[;] otherwise, an excellent investigation may be negated upon submission of the report.

> An articulate, well-written report is the most visible manifestation of a professional. It is often the only basis others have for determining the competence and work quality of both the individual officer and the organization he or she represents.

> Reports constitute a permanent record, which will last long after human memory has faded, and after-the-fact reality will be substantially based upon their contents. Unless an act or event is documented in an official report, its very existence may be questioned. Even the most conscientious work can be nullified by inadequate reporting. (no page)

Robinson's claims parallel the basic premise behind *The Blue Guide*. Writing is an important professional activity intricately linked to leadership, and in the case of especially police reports, the writing-leadership connection should never be underestimated. As Robinson makes clear, a police report is often the sole representation of the reporting officer and his/her investigation; as such, it perfectly demonstrates the Power of the Pen.

A good police report most obviously is written efficiently and effectively to support investigative work, but it also reflects positively upon the reporting officer and his/her police department. This positive reflection simultaneously builds professional image and promotes PR within a community or even across jurisdictional boundaries. Equally important, a good police report sets a professional example for others to follow. After all, a good report reflects the reporting officer's integrity, work ethic, team spirit, and thoroughness, and these are all leadership qualities that police officers should personally exhibit and promote in colleagues both up and down the chain of command. By setting personally high standards for report writing, then, a police officer is continually leading by example and helping to foster excellence in others.

With these basic leadership concepts in mind, Part II is divided into two chapters with one major goal: helping police officers write police reports efficiently and effectively so they can build self-image, promote good PR, and lead by example. Chapter Five examines the police report in a completely new way by defining it as a genre. Regardless of crime classification, all reports include the same basic genre features: first-person perspective, objective stance, highly specific and accurate content, chronological order, multiple audience, and correct format. Chapter Six builds on Chapter Five by providing three snapshots of police officers in the act of writing police reports. The snapshots begin with relevant background information, including educational level, law enforcement work history, and motivation for becoming a police officer, and they continue with specific information about each police officer's current position. The most important element, however, is a narrative description of each police officer conducting an investigation and then writing the corresponding police report. Together, these two chapters demonstrate the basics of writing police reports and the important role they play in police leadership.

CHAPTER FIVE

UNDERSTANDING THE POLICE REPORT AS GENRE

Reports must be an accurate articulation of the facts involved in the case. If the facts are inaccurate, then the case at hand is in jeopardy.

Sergeant David D. Wheatley
Warren County Sheriff's Department
Lebanon, Ohio

Leadership Objectives

- To recognize the police report as an important document, one promoting the professionalism of both the police officer and the police department.
- To understand the police report as a genre, a highly specialized type of document with six genre features: first-person perspective, objective stance, accurate and highly specific content, chronological order, multiple audience, and correct format.
- To know that the six genre features help establish the reporting officer's ethos, which is a leadership characteristic inspiring confidence and trust in others.
- To see the connection between report writing and police leadership.

Assess Yourself

Ask yourself the following questions:

- How would you describe police reports? What features do all police reports share?
- What is the purpose of a police report, and who is the audience?
- Should reports be written in first or third person? Is it okay to use the "all caps" key?
- Does grammar and usage really matter in police reports, as long as the information is accurate?
- Do you believe that writing reports enhance or detract from police officers' primary work responsibilities?

Genre is traditionally an academic term used to describe different literary forms, such as novels, short stories, poems, plays, and memoir (to name just a few). More recently, however, the meaning of the term has broadened across disciplines to include different types of professional communication, such as resumes, proposals, commendation letters, and year-end reports (to name just a few). It makes sense, then, that a police report is a genre too.

No other police writing handbook, however, has ever defined the police report as a genre; instead, the focus for teaching report writing has been on primarily content choices and correct format. As this chapter demonstrates, these two elements are central to writing reports, but they don't accurately reflect the complete complexity of police reports, which are more accurately described as having six genre features: first-person perspective, objective stance, accurate and highly specific content, chronological order, multiple audience, and correct format. This chapter fully explains and demonstrates each one.

It's important to note that, regardless of discipline or field, a person who knows how to break down any genre (academic, professional, or otherwise) into its basic and common characteristics, or genre features, will possess a fuller and more complex understanding of the genre in question. This understanding benefits the writer in two ways. First, it automatically and immediately enhances and streamlines the writing of documents in the particular genre. It makes sense, for example, that knowing the six genre features of police reports will enhance the quality of the report and the efficiency with which the officer writes it. There is, however, a second benefit "down the road" for the writer. Having analyzed the genre features of one document type, the writer is likely to gain the critical distance and awareness necessary to break down other types of documents, thereby enhancing the effectiveness and efficiency of future writing projects too.

THE SIX GENRE FEATURES OF POLICE REPORTS

As previously indicated, police reports are governed by six genre features: first-person perspective, objective stance, accurate and highly specific content, chronological order, multiple audience, and correct format. Understanding these features is the first step in learning to write police reports both effectively and efficiently.

First-Person Perspective

Police reports should be written in first-person perspective; that is, from an "I" point of view. Historically, police academies and police departments downplayed this fact about reports by teaching or requiring officers to write in third person, but that rhetorical practice is slowly changing and for logical reasons too. First, it doesn't fool audience members. Anyone can see that the person signing the report is the reporting officer. Second, third person does not reduce subjectivity or make the report "more objective." The bottom line is that a living, breathing human being is dispatched to a crime scene to conduct an investigation. There is no way to dispute it. It's important to stress, of course, that this person isn't *just anyone*. The person is a highly trained specialist who knows the laws, maintains critical distance, and has sworn to promote the public good. Still, this specialist is a person, and the report is written from his/her point of view. In fact, the report, itself, is grounded in the officer's field notes and personal memory of the investigation at hand.

Looking Back

Chapter One explains that effective writers know that writing is a process including planning, drafting, revising, and polishing. Consider the role that field notes play in the planning stage of writing a police report. Could a report be written without field notes?

To clarify first-person perspective, consider the following sentence pairs:

3rd Person.	The reporting officer was dispatched to 150 Wilts at 1400 hours.
1st Person.	I was dispatched to 150 Wilts at 1400 hours.
3rd Person.	Next, this officer interviewed the victim's aunt. She explained . . .
1st Person.	Next, I interviewed the victim's aunt. She explained . . .

Note: Writing in first person is usually faster for most police officers than writing in third person because first person "comes naturally." In every arena of public and personal life, police officers (like everyone else) communicate in first person.

Objective Stance

As the previous section makes clear, police reports are increasingly written from a first-person perspective. However, the investigating officer always maintains enough critical distance to take an objective stance. What does this mean? In the most simple and common sense understanding of the phrase, it means "just the facts" without emotion, prejudice, or bias. It means the officer is accurate, comprehensive, concrete, and fair-minded. As a result, a police report should inspire confidence in audience members and give them the true sense that they are reading a fair-minded and judicious description and/or assessment of the incident at hand. To clarify an objective stance, consider the following sentence pairs:

Subjective.	I would describe the suspect as a sloppy, overweight teenager.
Objective.	The suspect is a fifteen years old, approximately five feet two inches in height, and appearing to weigh over 200 pounds. He was dressed in torn blue jeans, a faded t-shirt, and a stained zip-up sweatshirt.
Subjective.	I could see the victim's car was totally demolished. It was a miracle that nobody was seriously injured or killed.

Objective: The hood of the victim's Ford Explorer was caved in, the windshield was shattered, and smoke was rising in large billows from the engine. Despite the extent of the vehicular damage, no serious injuries or fatalities took place.

What differences distinguish the subjective and objective versions of the previous sentences? Most obviously, biased descriptions, such as "sloppy," "overweight," and "totally demolished," are replaced with concrete facts, including height, weight, clothing, and damage specifications, but without being unnecessarily formal or "stuffy." Second, personal feelings ("It was a miracle that nobody was seriously injured or killed") are replaced with objective observations ("Despite the extent of the vehicular damage, there were no serious injuries or fatalities"). Last, unnecessary references to the investigating officer ("I could see" or "I would describe") are eliminated. In both cases, the context of the report establishes that the observations "belong" or "come from" the investigating officer.

For further clarification regarding unnecessary references to the investigating officer, consider an edited excerpt from an actual police report:

Writing Sample 5.1

At 2100 hours, Detective Jan Schultz called to say Peter Anderson's vehicle was under surveillance on Western Avenue. At 2140 hours, she called back and reported that Anderson had wrecked his car running from police. At 2300 hours, Schultz reported Peter Anderson was in custody and being transported to the police station (he was first taken to the hospital and released).

Looking Back

Does the reporting officer appear to have good ethos? In other words, do you trust that he/she is providing an accurate assessment of what took place? Why? If not, what other information in the report might give this impression?

Writing Sample 5.1 is written from a first-person perspective, even though it doesn't specifically use the first-person pronoun. The overarching context of the police report would make clear that the investigating officer received three phone calls from Detective Jan Schultz; during each call, the detective provided the officer with an update on the suspect.

Looking Back

Reread Writing Sample 5.1 and notice the first three sentences. Explain the comma rule in the beginning of the first three sentences. Identify the FCA.

Looking Back

Reread Writing Sample 5.1 and consider these two variations of the same sentence:

- Schultz reported Peter Anderson was in custody and being transported to the police station (both were first taken to the hospital).
- Schultz reported Peter Anderson was in custody, and he was being transported to the police station (both were first taken to the hospital).

Why does the second sentence use a comma in the second line? Identify the FCA.

Note: Writing with an objective stance does not take any additional time. On the contrary, an objective stance becomes second nature to most police officers as a result of field training and the natural acculturation process into departmental life.

Accurate and Highly Specific Content

Even civilians know that police reports should include "just the facts." The question, of course, is which facts and why? The answer to this question is complicated because there are approximately twenty-five *primary class codes* representing different types of crimes, and each class code may have up to ten subcategories, depending on the specifics of the incident at hand. As one might expect, the police reports for each crime type require different content. For example, an officer must include weather/road conditions for a report documenting a car accident; however, that information would be irrelevant in the reporting of an assault or liquor violation. Similarly, an officer would indicate that photographs were taken at an arson or murder scene, but that detail would not be found in the police report of a driver's license or bad check violation.

Despite variations, however, all reports must establish *probable cause* that a law was broken, and it must identify the persons involved. In addition, the report should indirectly show that the reporting officer followed proper procedure and demonstrated professional conduct. To accomplish these objectives, all police reports—regardless of case classification—include the following:

- Date/Time of the Dispatch Call
- Identification of Responding Officer(s)
- Exact Location of the Incident
- Identification of Complainant(s), Victim(s), and/or Witness(es)
- Procedures followed by the Responding Officer(s),
- Interactions with Complainant(s), Victim(s), and Witness(es),
- Probable Cause (PC)
- Correct Crime Classification

To clarify, consider the content of this report written by Captain William Stewart of the New Philadelphia Police Department. Captain Stewart is an experienced police officer, and this report shows why. He has included all key content elements, even though the police report is only three paragraphs long.

Writing Sample 5.2

On October 24, 2006 at 2300, the New Philadelphia Police Department received a call from Tyler Owens. He stated that his sister, Tracy McGivens, had told him that her husband, Curtis McGivens, had thrown her against a wall.

Officer Finley and I responded to the call and made contact with the victim, Tracy McGivens (2234 South Madison), who advised that she and her husband, Curtis McGivens (2234 South Madison), had been arguing earlier and that the argument escalated to the point that Curtis grabbed her by the wrist and threw her against a wall. Tracy did have red marks on her upper chest, and her right wrist was slightly swollen. She advised that she wished to pursue charges and she submitted a written statement. In addition, Tracy signed the Domestic Violence Form.

Curtis was located a short time later by Officer Finley near the intersection of Davenport and Bancroft. He was transported to the police station and advised of his Miranda Rights, and he advised that he wanted to speak with an attorney prior to making any statement. He was booked into the New Philadelphia City Jail and is currently being held, pending an appearance in court.

Looking Back

How does Captain Stewart's police report help him lead by example?

Looking Back

Captain Stewart paraphrases comments instead of directly quoting. Using FCA #9, rewrite the passage so that either Tracy or Curtis McGivens is directly quoted.

Looking Back

Consider the individual paragraphs of Writing Sample 5.2 Is paragraph length monitored? Does each paragraph contain a topic sentence and then supporting information?

Chronological Order

Police reports are quickly and relatively easy to organize because they are written in chronological order, beginning with the dispatch call, continuing with the investigation, and ending with the conclusion of the investigation. In Part III, *The Blue Guide* explains that other kinds of police documents, such as commendations, reprimands, requests, and directives (to name just a few administrative documents), are more effectively written using other organizational patterns; however, the police report is designed to document a sequence of events, so chronological order is the logical choice.

Note: Some police departments have computer programs to assist officers in report writing. These programs prompt the reporting officer with electronic cues asking for specific kinds of information (such as interviews with victims or road conditions), depending on the crime classification. In these departments, officers receive specialized training to use the software so they are able to submit reports in a timely manner.

Many police officers use "military time" when documenting events in a police report, a practice consistent with the paramilitary values in the field of law enforcement (not unlike the hierarchical institutional structure and military job titles). As the following chart shows, midnight is 0000 hours in military time, and the morning hours are basically self-explanatory (0100 hours is 1:00 AM; 0400 hours is 4:00 AM). After noon, standard time is calculated by subtracting 1200 from the military hour (1400 hours—1200 = 2:00 PM; 2330 hours—1200 = 11:30 PM). Before long, however, military time becomes second nature to police officers as it does to military personnel, and these calculations won't be necessary.

Military Time vs. Standard Time

0100 hours	1:00 AM	1300 hours	1:00 PM
0200 hours	2:00 AM	1400 hours	2:00 PM
0300 hours	3:00 AM	1500 hours	3:00 PM
0400 hours	4:00 AM	1600 hours	4:00 PM
0500 hours	5:00 AM	1700 hours	5:00 PM
0600 hours	6:00 AM	1800 hours	6:00 PM
0700 hours	7:00 AM	1900 hours	7:00 PM
0800 hours	8:00 AM	2000 hours	8:00 PM
0900 hours	9:00 AM	2100 hours	9:00 PM
1000 hours	10:00 AM	2200 hours	10:00 PM
1100 hours	11:00 AM	2300 hours	11:00 PM
1200 hours	Noon	0000 hours	Midnight

Looking Back

Revisit Writing Samples 5.1 and 5.2, paying special attention to the military time listed and then recast it as "civilian time." Do you think the use of military time is important in the field of law enforcement?

Multiple Audiences

Professional communication is always written to a specific person or group of persons; however, the person or group identified in the document is unlikely to be the sole audience. Regardless of industry or field, most professional communication has multiple audiences, five to be precise: *the initial and gatekeeper audiences*, the *primary and secondary* audiences, and the *watchdog audience* (Locker 58). Police reports in the field of law enforcement are no exception.

The *initial audience* for a police report is a supervising officer, usually a sergeant or lieutenant. This ranked officer functions as both an *initial audience* and a *gatekeeper* by (a) reviewing the report, (b) determining if it will "hold up" in the courts, (c) considering if it is correct in crime classification, format, and language, and then (d) approving or rejecting it. If the report is rejected, the reporting officer has no choice: it must be revised, according to the supervisor's specifications. The procedure is that simple. Officers may remember voicing complaints or even arguing with a teacher over a paper or test answer back in school. In a police department, however, this conduct is unacceptable because police departments are strictly hierarchical, and all daily operations—including the writing of police reports—take place under a tight chain of command. In this command chain, the supervising officer has the right and responsibility to approve or reject reports, and it's the responding officer's job to accept the decision and comply. Period. Once the report is approved by the supervising officer, it is then forwarded up the chain of command to the chief or a designee, depending on the size of the police department. Regardless, the report is carefully critiqued once again before final approval takes place. Note: In some departments, police reports are made available at roll call

Looking Back

As Chapter One explains, a hallmark of effective writers is understanding that writing is a process and that writing is a developmental skill. How might a supervising officer's critique of an individual report influence a reporting officer's writing processes? How might that same supervisor's critiques overtime positively influence the reporting officer's writing development?

After the initial and/or the gatekeeper audience(s) is the *secondary audience*: the Prosecutor's Office, which is the head law enforcement agency in any county. The prosecutor or a designee is the first person to read the report outside of the police department. It's the prosecutor's job to review the report to ensure that probable cause exists for an arrest; if it does exist, the prosecutor either authorizes the arrest (if it has already taken place) or prepares a criminal complaint and warrant. If the report doesn't demonstrate probable cause, then the prosecutor may request additional information from the reporting officer(s). In this way, the prosecutor is both a gatekeeper and a secondary audience. In addition to the Prosecutor's Office, however, there are other secondary audiences, including the court magistrate, the judge at the preliminary hearing, and the defense attorney. Like the prosecutor, each of these parties is interested in ensuring that (a) probable cause exists, (b) that the person named in the report and/or arrest warrant is the right person, and (c) that the responding officer followed proper procedure.

The *primary audience* for most police reports is the trial judge and/or jury. After all, the purpose of a report is to document a case investigation for court presentation or prosecution. Not all cases go to court, but reporting officers must always write reports with judges and/or juries in mind, in the event that the case does result in either a criminal or civil trial (or both). It's important to remember that in most cases, the officer's field notes have been shredded or otherwise destroyed, so the police report is the sole documentation of the case investigation. If the reporting officer can't be present during court, the report represents the officer and the police department, providing a crucial piece of evidence in the court proceedings. If present for the trial, the reporting officer may be allowed to refer to the police report to prepare for the hearing, so the report functions as field notes or "memory jogs."

In addition to the primary, secondary, and initial/gatekeeper audiences, there is one more: the *watchdog audience*. Watchdog audiences have no authority over a document; however, they do possess potential political, social, and economic power, and they pay careful attention to the document in question (Locker 58). For police reports, the watchdog audience comes into play primarily from the Freedom of Information Act. Because of this act, the primary watchdog is the media in all of its forms: newspapers, magazines, television, radio, and internet. In turn, the general public also functions as watchdogs.

Correct Format

Police reports must be submitted in the proper format, which may vary from one police department to another. In general, however, you should be aware of the following:

- **Standard Form.** Many police departments (especially larger departments) have created a standard form for police reports. On this form, there are typically two sections. The first section is a simple series of blanks located at the top of the page for basic information, such as date/time, responding officer, crime classification, location, and the complainant's name. These blanks allow audience members to see at a glance the highlights of the report. The second section is a large open "white space" for the police narrative, itself. The opening of the narrative, often referred to as the *summary information*, should repeat exactly what is listed in the blanks above, except in sentence form. Note: If departments don't use a standard form, officers should still strive for a two-part report, with the basic information, such as date/time, responding officer, crime classification, and complainant's name, highlighted at the top of the page followed by the narrative.

- **Supplemental Reports.** In complex cases and even some simple cases, it is often necessary to submit supplemental reports. These supplements might document individual interviews or follow-up procedures of any kind. These reports are stand-alone documents, but they work in conjunction with the other report(s) to document an investigation.

- **Handwritten vs. Typed.** In general, police reports should be typed. Doing so automatically renders the report more accessible and professional. In many police departments, however, computers/typewriters are not available to officers; officers in these departments should legibly print their police reports.

- **Spacing Conventions.** Police reports are single spaced documents *with double spacing between paragraphs* (a must!). This practice saves paper, and it is consistent with other professional communication documents. Don't ever submit a report comprised of one huge paragraph; on the other hand, don't submit reports comprised of a several one- to two-sentence paragraphs either (see Chapter Four for more information on paragraph length and boundaries).

- **Complete Sentences.** Police reports are written in complete sentences. Because of time constraints and other pressing obligations, it is tempting to complete reports with clipped phrases, but this is not a professional practice. Doing so makes the report appear more like field notes than an official report. Similarly, remember that all grammar/usage rules apply. See Part I for a review of the top twenty errors and strategies for writing concise sentences.

- **"All Caps" Key.** All capitalization rules (see Part I) apply in police reports. Most importantly, don't ever submit a police report written entirely in capital letters. Doing so reduces the professional appearance of both the report and the officer, and—thanks to email etiquette—may imply that the reporting officer is angry. Note: Some departments set computers so that officers have no choice but to write computers using "all caps." Ranked officers in these departments should strive to change this practice.

- **Standard Abbreviations.** Historically, police academies and police departments have taught and encouraged the use of abbreviations in police reports. It is important to remember, however, that police reports are formal documents, and abbreviations reduce formality. In other words, the use of abbreviations, though widespread in report writing, is an inconsistent practice. Moreover, writing words as abbreviations really doesn't save the responding officer a great deal of time, contrary to popular belief. If an officer does use abbreviations in a police report, it's important to use solely standard abbreviations.

- **Appropriate Signatures.** The reporting officer always signs the report, and so does his/her immediate supervisor. In most departments, the chief or a designee also signs. All three signatures confirm the accuracy and integrity of the police report.

Looking Back

How would using proper format help to build a police officer's professional self-image, promote PR, and lead by example? How does proper format provide evidence of high reporting standards?

THE SIX GENRE FEATURES AND POLICE LEADERSHIP

The six genre features—first-person perspective, objective stance, specific and highly accurate content, chronological order, multiple audience, and correct format—work together to establish *the ethos* of the reporting officer. Don't let the word, ethos, scare you! Ethos may be an ancient Greek term, but it's still relevant today, is widely used among writing specialists, and is closely related to leadership, especially police leadership. Ethos refers to that important quality or characteristic in a person inspiring confidence and trust in audience members, which is so crucial in the field of law enforcement. Audience members hear or, in the case of police reports, read the person's message and automatically have "a good feeling" about the person, intuitively sensing integrity, diligence, substance, and fair-mindedness: the characteristics that police officers exhibit and promote in colleagues both up and down the chain of command.

Ethos is an important leadership quality for writing literally every kind of police document; however, ethos is especially important in police reports. Why? It takes only a moment to explain. In writing other kinds of administrative police documents, officers may use *pathos* (emotional appeals) and/or *logos* (logical appeals) to persuade audience members into granting approval, taking action, or following procedure (as three good examples). Not so in police reports. In police reports, the purpose is not to persuade audience members in the traditional sense of the word. Instead, the writer's purpose is to report facts as a sequence of events in an honest and believable way, and this purpose requires that the reporting officer be a credible source. In short, it requires ethos.

Looking Back

Revisit Michael Robinson's claims regarding police reports in the Introduction of this chapter. Discuss his claims in relation to the concept of ethos.

Looking Back

Ethos is that characteristic in a person inspiring confidence and trust in others. Consider the importance of a police officer's ethos in light of the five multiple audiences—gatekeeper and initial audiences, primary and secondary audiences, and watchdog audiences—described in this section. Connect your discussion to police leadership.

To continue learning about reports, ethos, and police leadership, keep reading. Chapter Six builds upon these concepts with three snapshots of actual police officers in the act of writing police reports. The reports demonstrate the six genre features outlined in this chapter, and they make clear the relationship between the written word and police leadership.

Chapter Review

Police reports are the most common documents written in the field of law enforcement, and they are, arguably, the most important document because they provide the leadership foundation for any department.

Police reports provide an archived record of an investigation, one that lasts long after human memory fails. If a report is completed inaccurately, the investigative work is, at best, seriously compromised and, at worst, rendered null and void

Police reports are a specific genre with six genre features: first-person perspective, objective stance, accurate & highly specific content, chronological order, multiple audiences, and correct format. These six genre features help the writer to establish *ethos*, that quality in a person that inspires confidence and trust.

Well written reports help to build a police officer's professional self image, promote PR, and lead by example.

For Discussion

1. What are the six genre features of police reports? How does knowledge of the genre features increase efficiency and effectiveness?
2. Name the five multiple audiences.
3. What is probable cause? Why is it essential for police reports to establish it?
4. Why should police reports document the responding officer's procedure and professionalism?
5. Does it really matter whether police reports are grammatically correct? As long as the ideas are clear, what difference does correct grammar make?
6. What is the difference between first- and third-person perspectives? What is the rationale for using first-person perspective for police reports? Why was third-person traditionally required for police reports?
7. Have you ever been a complainant or witness to a crime? If yes, reflect upon that experience, especially the actions of the responding police officer(s). Did you ever read the corresponding police report? If yes, what do you remember about it? If no, try to imagine what the officer would have included.
8. Depending on its quality, how might a police report build or break a police officer's self-image? How might it enhance or eradicate PR? How might it help or hurt in leading by example?

TEST YOURSELF

Practice Exercise 5.1

Read the supplemental report written by Chief Dino Carozza of the Orrville Police Department and then answer the questions following it.

Supplemental Report

I created a photo line-up comprised of six people, including suspect Ben Bernard, and each photograph was marked with a number: Tom Sims (#1), Taylor Ians (#2), William Pohlerman (#3), Tom Sims (#4), Adam Morey (#5), and Andrew Weller (#6).

I made contact with Manager Sally Jones at the Corner Store at 0915 hours on January 2, 2004. I asked Ms. Jones to view the array of photographs, advising her that the robbery suspect may or may not be depicted. She viewed the photo line up and within five seconds pointed to the Photograph #4 (Tom Sims) and stated that he was the assailant. I thanked Ms. Jones for her time, and I advised her that she would be kept informed regarding the progress of the case.

Upon returning to headquarters, I contacted Prosecutor Nancy Burkett informed her of the results regarding the positive identification of the robbery suspect by Sally Jones. Prosecutor Burkett requested that I interview Tom Sims and attempt to obtain a confession. I contacted Sims by telephone that same day, and he agreed to meet with me at headquarters on January 2, 2004 at 1000 hours.

Questions

1. This police report is known as a supplemental report. Based upon its content, what kind of report does it supplement? What other reports might follow?
2. What is the crime classification, and how does the report establish probably cause? Why does the responding officer include the victim's timeframe in selecting a photograph?
3. What procedure did the responding officer follow? Why did he include the list of people depicted in the line-up and his contact with the Prosecutor's Office?
4. Does the police report demonstrate the six genre features? Identify key words and phrases that support your answer.
5. Is the responding officer professional and courteous in his dealing with the victim? If yes, how is this attitude documented in the report?
6. Does this police report provide a positive image of the writer and his department? Does it help to establish ethos? Will it allow him to lead by example? If yes, how?

Practice Set 5.2

Read the police report written by Sergeant Jack Hall of the Avon Lake Police Department and then answer the questions following it.

On August 15 at 0900 hours, I met with John Lalone and his attorney, Bill Proctor, regarding his involvement in this case. Lalone informed me that he had known Craig Swan since elementary school and Alex Sullivan since junior high school. He only knows Swan through his relationship with Craig's brother—Dan. Lalone stated that he has never committed any criminal acts with either of the other subjects, nor has he abused controlled substances with them.

I asked Lalone to describe his day on August 1 and explain chronologically how he came to be arrested by Avon Lake officers. Lalone indicated that he reported for work at 0800 that day and returned home at 1700. After arriving home, he ate and showered and went to Sullivan's home at approximately 1830. Lalone stated he was at Sullivan's home for about two hours when Craig and Dan Swan arrived. Lalone stated that Craig Swan initiated a conversation about getting a lot of money from a bowling alley and began to discuss a plan on how to steal it. Lalone stated that they left Sullivan's home shortly after 2030 to head for Avon Lake where Craig continued to discuss the plan in the car—mostly with Dan. Dan was driving his own vehicle with Craig seated in the front passenger seat, Sullivan in the left rear seat, and Lalone in the right rear seat..

Lalone stated they arrived at the local bowling alley at exactly 2003 (he had glanced at his watch), and Craig was angry that they might have arrived too late; Craig had indicated that a woman always brought the bank deposit to her car at the same time each night. Lalone stated that he, Sullivan, and Craig exited the vehicle and Dan went to park his vehicle in nearby lot. Lalone stated that Craig showed him and Sullivan where the exit to the bowling alley was, where the victim would exit, and where her vehicle would be located. According to Lalone, the victim walked out of the bowling alley, just as Craig had previously stated and she left the bag at the side of her vehicle. Lalone stated that he ran toward her vehicle as instructed, grabbed the bag, and ran around the bowling alley to the woods on the north side of the building. According to Lalone, he heard sirens and voices approaching his location shortly thereafter, so he dropped the bag and went into the woods to hide.

While in the woods, Lalone stated that he received several phone calls from Sullivan's cell phone, but he did not answer the calls until he consented to do so in the presence of police (see transcript of call in other supplements of this report).

Questions

1. What is the case classification for this supplemental report, and how does it help to establish probable cause? What other reports might also be included in this investigation?
2. Why does the report mention that an attorney was present when he didn't appear to say anything?
3. Does the report demonstrate the six genre features?
4. How does the report provide evidence of strong police leadership? Does it provide evidence of positive self-image? Does it help to establish ethos? Will the report help the writer lead by example?

Practice Set 5.3

Read the police report written by Sergeant Donald Durst of the Lake County Sheriff's Office and then answer the questions following it.

On 7-29 at 1712 hours, I was dispatched to 655 Fancher Street in reference to a criminal mischief complaint. Upon arrival at 1715 hours, I spoke with the complainant/homeowner, Mr. Petrick, who advised that his family had been out of town from 7-25-05 until about an hour previously at approximately 1600 hours. At this time, Mr. Petrick discovered that his fifteen-year-old daughter's bedroom window (located on the northeast corner of the home) had been struck with at least two eggs. I observed no damage caused by the eggs; however, the window and another one (located on the north side of the home) had been previously damaged by a BB gun. This damage was documented in Report # 05-345.

I spoke with Mr. Petrick for approximately twenty minutes about the two incidents. Mr. Petrick indicated that he had no idea who was responsible, but I advised him that they were probably not "random acts" because (a) the two incidents were both directed at the same bedroom window and (b) the house is located on a dead-end street. Mr. Petrick concurred, but he indicated that his daughter is, to his knowledge, not having problems with anyone. Moreover, he is hesitant to accuse anyone without proof.

I suggested the following to Mr. Petrick. First, I suggested that he contact the parents of his daughter's friends and explain the situation to them; perhaps these parents would be willing to discuss the incident with their children. Second, I suggested that his daughter ask her friends to keep their ears open; perhaps they'll overhear another student bragging about damaging the Breedlove residence. Mr. Petrick advised that he would take both suggestions. He also advised that if he obtained any useful information, he would contact me.

I left the Petrick residence at 1740 hours. No action needed.

Questions

1. What is the crime classification for this report, and how does the report establish probable cause?
2. The responding officer took no action, and there doesn't appear to be any supplemental report. Why?
3. The report documents that the officer was professional and respectful of the Petrick family: true or false? Explain.
4. Why didn't the officer interview Mr. Petrick's daughter?
5. Notice that the report is divided into four paragraphs. Analyze the paragraph boundaries in terms of the following elements: (a) topic sentence, (b) paragraph unity, and (c) paragraph length.
6. How does this report provide evidence of strong police leadership?

MyCompLab—Optional Exercises and Activities

As the homepage shows, MyCompLab is divided into three sections: Grammar, Writing, and Research.

- Under Writing, click Writing Activities and then View All Activities by Writing Purpose. Finally, select Writing to Describe and Writing to Inform. Read both sections carefully and then answer these questions: (a) How would you characterize what it means to describe or inform in writing? (b) What is the relationship between writing to describe and/or inform with writing police reports? (c) How are they all alike, and how are they all different? (d) Read Writing to Reflect (found in the same general section) and compare reflective writing with report writing. In answering each of theses questions, keep in mind the six genre features of police reports and be prepared to share your answers in small groups, class discussions, or written form, as your instructor requests.
- Under Writing, click Model Documents and then select the recommendation, the instructions, the proposal, and/or the report, as your instructor requests. Read each document carefully and compare its purpose, audience, and format to that of police reports. In addition, do a comparison that takes into consideration the six genre features of police reports.
- Under Grammar, click Quotations (found under Basic Grammar), Bias in Language/Sexist Language (found under Usage and Style), and Voice – Active and Passive (found under Sentence Editing). Complete the exercises in these sections, as your instructor requests, and then consider how the concepts would strengthen police reports.
- Under Grammar and or Writing, revisit any of the exercises/activities regarding paragraphs (see the MyCompLab exercises identified at the end of Chapter Four). Are the concepts and strategies relevant to report writing? If yes, why and how? More specifically, how can police officers apply paragraphing these concepts and strategies to police writing?

CHAPTER SIX

CELEBRATING THREE POLICE OFFICERS

Good officers will check their police reports to ensure that the facts are accurate and each sentence is error-free.

Detective Sergeant Jeffrey S. Pickler
Central Michigan University Police Department
Mt. Pleasant, Michigan

Leadership Objectives

- To reinforce the Chapter Five Objectives: (1) Recognize the police report as an important document, one promoting the professionalism of both the police officer and the police department. (2) Understand the police report as a genre, a highly specialized kind of document with six genre features: first-person perspective, objective stance, accurate and highly specific content, chronological order, multiple audience, and correct format. (3) See the connection between police reports and leadership.
- To gain a fuller understanding for the process of writing a police report; to see the police report as a logical extension of a police officer's investigation.

Assess Yourself

Ask yourself the following questions:

- What do you believe is the relationship between an investigation and the corresponding police report?
- What do you suppose are the steps in writing a police report? How do reporting officers plan, draft, revise, and polish their reports?
- How efficiently must reports be written?
- How much report writing do police officers really do? How does report writing influence overall job performance?
- Should police officers take pride in report writing? What happens when they do? What happens when they don't?

Chapter Five introduced a new concept: the police report as genre. This concept posits that all police reports—regardless of crime classification or individual police officer/department—share the same six genre features: first-person perspective, objective stance, specific and highly accurate content, chronological order, multiple audience, and proper format. Moreover, Chapter Five asserts that these six genre features work together to help establish the police officer's ethos, which is a leadership quality or characteristic in a person inspiring confidence and trust in others. Even further, the chapter argues that good police reports help to build a person's self-image, promote PR, and they also assist police officers in leading by example.

Chapter Six complements Chapter Five by providing snapshots of three police officers (representing rural, suburban, and urban departments) in the act of writing police reports. They are Under Sheriff John Vinson of the Isabella County Sheriff's Department, Deputy Sheriff John Chasse of the Delaware County Sheriff's Office, and Lieutenant Colonel Margaret Rose of the University of Cincinnati Police Department. The snapshots all begin with relevant background information regarding the police officers in question and their current positions, and they continue with a narrative description of a dispatch call, including the investigation and important details about writing the report, followed by the corresponding police report.

Together, the snapshots are designed to demonstrate the six genre features described in Chapter Five. In addition, they provide a window into the writing lives of three police officers, helping *Blue Guide* readers understand the process of writing police reports efficiently and effectively and the important role those reports play in establishing the leadership status of the individual officers.

SNAPSHOT #1: INVESTIGATING A CASE OF DOMESTIC VIOLENCE

JOHN VINSON, UNDER SHERIFF
ISABELLA COUNTY SHERIFF'S DEPARTMENT
MT. PLEASANT, MICHIGAN

With over ten years in law enforcement, Under Sheriff John Vinson has had ample experience both writing and critiquing police reports. In this snapshot, he demonstrates the importance of staying calm during a domestic violence investigation and of carefully documenting interviews during any investigation.

Background Information

Full Name: John Nathaniel Vinson

Education
PhD (2004), Western Michigan University
MA in Administration (1998) Central Michigan University
BS in Business Administration (1993) Central Michigan University
Diploma (1989), Southfield High School

Previous Law Enforcement Positions:
Sergeant, Central Michigan University Police Department
Police Officer, Central Michigan University Police Department

Off-Duty Interests
During off-duty hours, I enjoy traveling, reading, and exercising. Most importantly, though, I like spending time with my family.

Motivation for Becoming a Police Officer
I was looking for a profession that provided an opportunity to have a positive impact in the community. In addition, I wanted a job where the tasks were different everyday, but extremely fun and often times challenging.

Looking Back

Does Under Sheriff Vinson's background information provide evidence of good ethos? What specific details about his profile give you this impression?

Current Position

ICSD Profile/Mission Statement

Isabella County covers 586 square miles and has a population of approximately 65,000 residents. Mount Pleasant, the county seat, is its largest community, playing host to many Central Michigan University students and Soaring Eagle Casino guests.

The Isabella County Sheriff's Department is led by Sheriff Leo Mioduszewski. He is responsible for a budget of approximately $5,000,000 and commands sixty-five employees assigned to eight different divisions. The Isabella County Sheriff's Department is committed to improving the quality of life, promoting peace and resolving problems through ongoing, work partnerships with the citizens of our community.

Job Description

As the under sheriff, I am second in command. I plan, organize and direct the daily operations of sixty-five employees in the eight departmental divisions, and I plan/monitor an annual budget of $5,000,000 (including training and grant distribution). In addition, my responsibilities include personnel issues, including hiring, promoting, and negotiating grievances/contracts, with three different employee groups (one non-union/two union). Last, I am responsible for writing, updating, and reviewing departmental policy and procedure.

Writing Responsibilities at Work

In addition to writing, updating, and reviewing departmental policy and procedure, I have many other writing responsibilities, most of them administrative in nature. To name just a few, I routinely write memos and/or letters internally to employees and externally to various constituencies on a variety of topics, and I also conduct different types of investigations, which requires completing comprehensive reports in many forms and for multiple audiences. In addition, I annually write a year-end report showcasing the department's accomplishments for the County Commission, and I also write grants on a fairly regular basis. These are just a few examples.

Looking Back

According to Under Sheriff Vinson, Isabella County is the home to Central Michigan University and the Soaring Eagle Casino. Imagine a case scenario requiring police action in either setting.

Next, consider the following questions about the case scenario:

- What is the Big Picture? In other words, who is the victim, what crime was committed, who are the suspects, and are there witnesses?
- What role would university officials or tribal members play? Would they be a initial/gatekeeper audience, a primary/secondary audience, or a gatekeeper audience? Why do you think so, and what would the ramifications be?

Looking Back

Reconsider Under Sherrif Vinson's writing responsibilities. How could his writing promote leadership initiatives, such as building self-image, enhancing PR, promoting policies/procedures, or increasing esprit de corps?

Snapshot #1
Police Work in Action: An Incident of Domestic Violence

On July 11, 2005, I was working in my office when I overhead Isabella County Central Dispatch tone out a domestic assault in progress at a location in Isabella County, Michigan. Since there were no road patrol deputies available, I responded to the location. I was assisted by two officers: one from the Sherman Townships Marshal's Office and one from the Saginaw Chippewa Tribal Police Department.

The officer from the Marshal's Office arrived at the location first and separated the parties. He obtained their names and dates of births, and he verified that no one was injured. Once I arrived, I took over the investigation. The male suspect was temporarily placed in the rear of my patrol vehicle, where he was read his Miranda rights. He subsequently waived his rights and agreed to speak with me. After interviewing him, I spoke to the victim, who was still inside the residence. During both interview, I took field notes, and the two main questions I asked attempted to find out the nature of their relationship and whether any physical violence had occurred.

There was probable cause, and so after the interviews, the male suspect was arrested on two counts: Domestic Violence and Disconnecting a Phone Line. I transported him to Isabella County Jail where he was booked and lodged on the charges.

After the suspect was processed in the jail, I returned to my office to complete the report. I utilized our records management system called AICS to complete the report. The system is set up where I enter all names in various name fields, as well as the charge codes and other relevant information. Once that is completed, the system allows me to open an attached word document, which automatically provides all of the necessary headings in order to complete the actual police report. For each heading, I typed in the necessary information.

After completing the report, I typed out the warrant request and affidavit. The warrant request is the document requesting formal charges, and the affidavit supports the rationale for the charges. The police report, warrant request, and affidavit were forwarded to the Prosecutor's Office for further review.

Looking Back

When does Under Sheriff Vinson establish probable cause?

Looking Back

Did Under Sheriff Vinson follow proper procedure in conducting this investigation? What does he specifically say that makes you think so?

Looking Back

What information does Under Sheriff Vinson provide regarding his writing process? What is his planning strategy, and how do you predict technology influences his drafting, revising, and polishing?

How does technology help Under Sheriff Vinson to be an efficient, as well as an effective, writer when it comes to police reports? How does his extensive experience in report writing influence his efficiency?

How seriously do you think Under Sheriff Vinson takes the writing of police reports?

Snapshot #1
The Police Narrative for a Domestic Assault and Disconnecting a Telephone

Information:

On 10/11/05, Isabella County Central Dispatch toned out a domestic in progress, and Sherman 1 Marshall Hooker, Tribal Police Officer Foco, and I responded to the location. We arrived at the location and conducted the investigation. While conducting the investigation, we observed a 3-month-old child in the residence and another small child involved in the altercation. David Davidson was subsequently arrested for Domestic Violence and Disconnecting a Phone Line.

Interview: Arrested

Sherman 1 verbally advised DAVIDSON of his Miranda rights, which he subsequently waived, and he agreed to speak with us. DAVIDSON stated he has been dating ANDERSON for about 2–3 years. He stated he believes the infant is his child, and he moved to Broomfield Township to be closer to the child. DAVIDSON advised that he was having an argument with ANDERSON on the front porch. He stated her son, JAMIE, tried to bite him and hit him with a baseball bat. DAVIDSON stated that all he tried to do was stop JAMIE from hitting him. He went on to say that ANDERSON got upset and started to make a phone call. He thought she was calling her ex-boyfriend so he took the phone from her right hand and disconnected the call. ANDERSON told him she was calling the police, but he figured the police would call back. DAVIDSON said that he believed he had the right to monitor who uses his phone since he pays the bill. DAVIDSON denied ever hitting her.

Interview: Victim Ann Anderson

ANDERSON stated she is married but has been dating DAVIDSON for about 2–3 years. She stated that they have lived together in the past, and she believes DAVIVDSON is the father of her infant child. Her other child has another father. She reported that she and DAVIDSON have had arguments throughout their relationship and yesterday, 10/10/05, and today was no different. She indicated on 10/10/05, around noon, DAVIDSON and her daughter, JAMIE, got into an argument. During the argument, she told DAVIDSON to leave her daughter alone. ANDERSON and DAVIDSON then started arguing. During the argument, he threw her into the kitchen counter, which resulted in a bruise on her right hip. She stated that DAVIDSON also struck JAMIE in the right shoulder during this incident.

On 10/11/05, ANDERSON stated that the arguing continued. Around 1400 hours, ANDERSON stated DAVIDSON locked both JAMIE and her out of the house. During this timeframe, DAVIDSON stayed inside of the residence with the infant child. After about an hour, DAVIDSON let them back in and ANDERSON told him she wanted to leave. DAVIDSON started shoving her and JAMIE down the hallway towards to door. She stated she grabbed the phone and dialed 911. DAVIDSON then ripped the phone out of her hand. She went outside and DAVIDSON threatened to knock her fucking teeth down her throat, and then he tried to shove her back into the house. ANDERSON then grabbed JAMIE'S hand and ran to the Good Times Party Store where she re-contacted Central Dispatch.

Interview with Victim Jamie Anderson:

JAMIE stated his mom and DAVIDSON argue all the time. She stated that DAVIDSON hit his mom with his fist and struck her in the right shoulder.

Injuries:

ANDERSON had a visible bruise on the crest of her right hip. The bruise was approximately 4 x 2 inches in size and was purple in color.

JAMIE ANDERSON had minor marks on her right shoulder area.

Enforcement Action:

DAVIDSON was placed under arrest, transported to ICSD where he was booked, fingerprinted and lodged on the charges of Domestic Violence and Disconnecting a Telephone.

Prosecutor's Office:

I submitted the original report, a warrant request and an affidavit to the Isabella County Prosecutor's Office requesting formal charges on MOORE.

Status:

Closed

Looking Back

Analyze this police report in terms of probable cause, officer conduct, and the six genre features:

- First-Person Perspective
- Objective Stance
- Accurate & Highly Specific Content
- Chronological Order
- Multiple Audience
- Correct Format

Looking Back

Does Under Sheriff Vinson's police report help him establish good ethos? How does his report help him lead by example?

Looking Back

Does Under Sheriff Vinson follow the ten FCAs (Chapter Two) in his police report, and do you find his sentence structure clear, concise, and to the point (Chapter Three)? How do the headings required by his department influence paragraph length?

SNAPSHOT #2: INVESTIGATING A ROUTINE TRAFFIC STOP

LYLE CHASSÉ, DEPUTY SHERIFF
DELAWARE COUNTY SHERIFF'S OFFICE
DELAWARE, OHIO

A former military police officer and now a deputy sheriff, Lyle Chassé has been working in the field of law enforcement for nearly twenty years. In this snapshot, he demonstrates how routine traffic stops can quickly change and become far more complicated. The traffic stop in question took place when Deputy Sheriff Chassé was a lieutenant for the Galion Police Department.

Background Information

Full Name: Lyle Andrew Chassé

Education
Police Academy, North Central State College (96)
Police Academy, North Central Texas University (95)
US Military Police Academy (1990)
Kettering High School (1988)

Previous Positions in Law Enforcement
Lieutenant, Galion Police Department
Patrol Officer, Lexington Police Department
Patrol Officer, US Army Military Police

Off-Duty Interests
During off-duty hours, I enjoy family time, especially camping trips with my wife and four children. I also enjoy weight lifting and boxing.

Motivation for Becoming a Police Officer
As a young man, I joined the military police and became hooked on the unpredictability of the day-to-day functions in the law enforcement field. After leaving the military, I wanted to serve the community in which I was raising my children.

Looking Back

Deputy Sheriff Chassé is clearly an upwardly mobile police officer; what leadership characteristics do you believe helped him advance and what role do you think effective writing played in all of his promotions? Before answering this question, revisit Scenario #2 in Chapter One.

Current Position

DCSO Profile/Mission Statement

Delaware County, which is home to over 100,000 residents, covers 459 square miles and is located approximately twenty-five miles north of Columbus, which is the state capitol. The county seat is Delaware, and Delaware County is reportedly one of the fastest growing counties in Ohio and the entire USA.

The Delaware County Sheriff's Office is led by Sheriff Al Myers. He supervises more than eighty sworn officers in six different divisions. The Delaware County Sheriff's Office is committed to providing quality service to its residents.

Job Description

My primary responsibility is to patrol the streets of Delaware County to ensure the protection of the citizens and their property. In addition, I am responsible for the following: maintaining the jail and transporting prisoners, preparing cases and paperwork for court, and serving warrants and civil papers.

Writing Responsibilities at Work

For every case where an arrest or even a possible arrest takes place, I must write a report to explain what occurred, when it occurred, why there is a suspect, and what I did about the case when I received the complaint. All evidence must be collected and a separate report written for each item. At least 90% of my on-the-job writing is report writing.

Looking Back

Deputy Sheriff Chassé claims that reporting writing represents 90% of his on-the-job responsibilities. Compare this observation with Michael Robinson's claims regarding the importance of report writing in the introduction to Chapter Five.

Looking Back

How seriously do you believe that Deputy Sheriff Chassé takes report writing? What makes you think so? How would sloppy or inaccurate report writing influence his job performance? How important would writing efficiency be?

Looking Back

Draw a relationship between Deputy Sheriff Chassé's report writing and his primary responsibilities, which he claims is to "ensure the protection of the citizens and their property." Is there a relationship between his writing and leadership responsibilities?

Snapshot #2
Police Work in Action: A Routine Traffic Stop Becomes an OMVI

I began my tour of duty on January 13th, 2001 as usual: I got into my cruiser and checked to make sure all the equipment was turned on and functioning. I started the cruiser, checked the emergency lights, looked for damage on the cruiser, turned on the radar system, put the tape in the VCR, checked the camera system, and finally checked the laptop computer to make sure it's working too. It's amazing how far technology has come. When I first started in law enforcement, all I carried in my cruiser was a handheld radar unit, but now I have a computer, along with a camera system to record everything I do and say. I hear a lot of people say how technology is supposed to make a person's life easier, but is this really true for the field of law enforcement?

At any rate, I found myself later that night driving behind a Toyota truck, but I couldn't read the license plate because of a bright white light bulb facing above it. Even when I drove a little closer (twenty feet), I still couldn't read it, and I noticed too that the window tint was quite dark. Both the light bulb and the tinted windows are traffic offenses, so I made the traffic stop; that's when I saw a third offense: the license plate was half blocked by the bumper too.

The truck pulled over to the roadside, and I parked directly behind it. Then I exited my cruiser, walked to the driver window, and spoke to the driver, who was a person later a moment later as Matthew Donaldson. Following standard procedure, I asked him for his driver's license, registration, and proof of insurance. As Donaldson handout over the papers, though, I smelled alcohol on his breath and I saw a 12 pack of unopened beer on the passenger seat, so I asked him to step out of the truck and submit to standard field sobriety tests, which he agreed to do. As the police report shows, it's important to explain each test carefully and note results, which I did. Because Donaldson failed two of the three tests, I could not allow him to drive home. He tried to call his sister, but nobody initially answered, so I suggested that Donaldson have a seat in the back of my cruiser.

While waiting for a warning tag for Donaldson, I saw that his license indicated he was under 21, and a check confirmed that he was, in fact, 20 years old, so I arrested him for OMVI. I handcuffed Donaldson (using double locks—an important procedure to follow and document) and then transported him to the station for processing. At the station, I read the

BMV form 2255 to Donaldson, and he agreed to take a BAC test; his results were .157 grams of alcohol per 210 liters of breath. I gave Donaldson a copy of the BMV form 2255 and then I issued a citation for OMVI and explained his mandatory court date. In addition, I issued a warning tag for white light to the rear, obstructed plate, and window tint. Donaldson was released to his sister, and the videotape from cruiser was placed into evidence. Pictures of beer were placed in the captain's mailbox to be placed with the police report.

To write the police report, I always begin by sitting for a moment and just thinking about the case. As this traffic stop shows, things happen fast on the streets and so if an officer doesn't collect his/her thoughts, the facts of the case may confuse defense attorneys. The two most important elements in a report are facts and details. Each report must have the elements of the crime, which are shown in the facts of the case. Details are also important. If a victim has injuries, for example, the person reading the report should be able to visualize them. Another key element is readability, a goal best accomplished by dividing a report into different paragraphs. Too many times, I find reports comprised of one big paragraph. This approach makes it extremely difficult to read by supervisors and prosecutors alike. The bottom line is that the best way to have credibility in courts is to write excellent reports.

Looking Back

As Chapter One explains, planning is an important part of the writing process, and Deputy Sheriff Chassé clearly agrees. What are his planning strategies? How do you predict good planning helps to save time in the long run?

Looking Back

Reconsider Deputy Sheriff Chassé's claims regarding the importance of details in police reports, and then read the following sentences (taken from Chapter Five):

Subjective: I would describe the suspect as a sloppy, overweight teenager.

Objective: The suspect is a fifteen year old, approximately five feet two inches in height and appearing to weigh over two hundred pounds. He was dressed in torn blue jeans, a faded t-shirt, and a stained zip-up sweatshirt.

Which version do you think Deputy Sheriff Chassé would prefer? Which version provides the clearer visual image for readers?

The objective version is clearly longer; however, would it necessarily require more time to write? If no, why not? If yes, is the additional time worth it for a police officer?

Snapshot #2
The Police Report for a Routine Traffic Stop and an OMVI

On January 13, 2001 at 0059 hours, I was driving behind a Toyota truck with a bright white light bulb facing to the rear, above the license plate (the light bulb was so bright that I could not see the license plate from twenty feet away), and I also saw that the window tint was very dark in the rear window. I made the traffic stop and this is when I saw that the plate was half blocked by the bumper.

I walked to the driver window and spoke to the driver—Matthew Donaldson—and asked for driver's license, registration, and proof of insurance. When Donaldson provided these papers, I smelled a moderate odor of alcohol on his breath and saw an unopened 12 pack of beer on the passenger seat. I asked Donaldson to step out of the car and submit to field sobriety tests, and he agreed.

I administered four tests. The first test explained and given was the Finger to Nose Test. Donaldson missed the tip of his nose twice with his left finger and once with his right finger, and he was swaying slightly to the left and the right throughout the procedure. The second test explained and given was the One Leg Stand, which Donaldson passed. The third test explained and given was the Horizontal Gaze Nysfagmus Test, and I received four clues. The last test explained and given was the Walk and Turn Test. On this test, Donaldson lost his balance a little while turning. Given results, I advised Donaldson that I could not allow him to drive and that someone would need to pick him up. He called his sister, but nobody answered the phone, so I suggested taking a seat in the back of my cruiser.

While waiting for the warning tag, I saw that Donaldson's license indicated he was under the age of twenty-one by one month, and a check confirmed he was still twenty years old, so I arrested him for OMVI, placed him in handcuffs with double locks, and transported him to the station, where I read him the BMV form 2255. He agreed to take the BAC test and registered .157 grams of alcohol per 210 liters of breath. As required, I provided Donaldson with a copy the BMV form, issued a citation for OMVI, and explained his mandatory court date. I also issued Donaldson a warning tag for white light to the rear, an obstructed license plate, and tinted windows. Donaldson was then released to his sister, Angela Donaldson.

I placed the videotape from the cruiser into evidence the photographs of beer into the Captain Seigenthal's mailbox to be filed with this report.

Looking Back

Analyze this police report in terms of probable cause, officer conduct, and the six genre features:

- First-Person Perspective
- Objective Stance
- Accurate & Highly Specific Content
- Chronological Order
- Multiple Audience
- Correct Format

Looking Back

Analyze Deputy Sheriff Chassé's paragraph boundaries. Revisit Chapter Four and determine whether his paragraph structure and length are appropriate. Do you agree with Deputy Sheriff Chassé that the multi-paragraph organization helps to make documents more readable?

Looking Back

How does Deputy Sheriff Chassé's police report suggest that he sets high personal standards for his own report writing? Does the report provide evidence of good ethos? Does it manifest good investigative work? If yes, in what ways, and how might they positively influence colleagues both up and down the chain of command?

SNAPSHOT #3:
INVESTIGATING AN ALARM DROP

MARGARET A. ROSE, LIEUTENANT COLONEL
UNIVERSITY OF CINCINNATI POLICE DEPARTMENT
CINCINNATI, OHIO

A veteran police officer, Lieutenant Colonel Margaret Rose has spent years writing and evaluating police reports in an urban setting. In this snapshot, she conducts an investigation of an alarm drop at a university business office. The report shows how potentially dangerous investigations can be.

Background Information

Full Name: Margaret Ann Rose

Education
BS in Physical Therapy (1999), University of Cincinnati
BS in Accounting (1983), University of Cincinnati
BS in Criminal Justice (1981), University of Cincinnati
Associates in Law Enforcement Technology (1979), University of Cincinnati
Diploma (1977), Our Lady of Angels

Previous Positions in Law Enforcement
Captain, UC Police Department
Administrative Lieutenant, UC Police Department
OIC, Crime Prevention, UC Police Department
Patrol Officer, Background Investigations, UC Police Department
Police Officer, UC Police Department

Off-Duty Interests
I do a lot of volunteer work. For example, I enjoy taking my dog to visit nursing homes (Delta Society/Pet Partners) and serving as a Eucharistic minister and in the Caring Companions Ministry at church. In addition, I like playing softball and volleyball, taking day trips to especially state parks, and following both the Reds and the Bengals.

Motivation for Becoming a Police Officer
When I was a little girl, a friend lived down the street and around the bend, so when either one of us walked home after dark, our mothers would come outside and watch us walk home. At the time, I remember thinking that I wanted to grow up and become a police officer so that I could help make streets safe so that parents wouldn't have to worry about their children walking home.

Looking Back

Does Lieutenant Colonel Rose have good ethos? What details about her profile help give you this impression?

Current Position

UCPD Profile/Mission Statement

The UCPD consists of a chief, assistant chief, three captains, eight lieutenants, fifty sworn police officers, and forty-three non-sworn security officers, as well as an auxiliary police officer component comprised of ten officers.

The UCPD mission is "To provide services that promote a safe, secure, and accommodating environment" to the university community. The vision is to "exceed customer needs and expectations, be an active partner in creating a vibrant and welcoming campus, and contribute to the prestige of the university." This vision is accomplished by utilizing our core values of PRIDE: professionalism, respect, integrity, dedication, and enthusiasm.

Job Description:

My basic function is to assist the chief in planning and directing police operations:

- Plan, direct, and analyze resources, oversee budget expenditures, and assign duties to police supervisors/officers, security officers and auxiliary officers.
- Develop policies/procedures and review criminal incidents reported daily; oversee internal/external police investigations.
- Establish employment requirements, promotions and allocations of personnel; hire, counsel and evaluate staff, and develop/maintain training programs.
- Advise deans, department heads, faculty, staff and students on safety and security matters; serve as liaison for security at the University Hospital..
- Serve as liaison for local/allied police agencies and criminal justice system.
- Interpret and enforce laws, rules and regulations; apprehends and arrests violators; testifies in court.

Writing Responsibilities at Work

In previous positions, I primarily wrote police reports, crime prevention programs/ brochures, and standard operating procedures. As administrative lieutenant and captain, I am responsible for checking reports. In addition, I also write proposals for short and long-range goals, and I carefully write e-mails to parents/students clarifying any type of concerns they may have.

Looking Back

Emails are often informal documents, and yet Lieutenant Colonel Rose writes them to UC parents/students with care. Imagine a Big Picture requiring her to be especially careful in purpose, diction, and format. Does this care require more time? If yes, is it time well spent? In general, how do you think writing processes change for email? In addition, how is the concept of multiple audiences complicated?

Looking Back

Lieutenant Colonel Rose has a broad range of job responsibilities. In which responsibilities do you suppose writing plays a major role?

Snapshot #3
Police Work in Action: Investigating an Alarm Drop

While on patrol at 0300 hours on November 16, 2003, I was dispatched for an alarm drop on the business office for football concessions. Officer Tom Cameron and I were both at least five minutes from the scene and, due to recent construction on the campus, it would not be easy to (a) gain access to the area and (b) cover all potential exits.

On our approach to the building, neither of us noticed anything out of the ordinary. There were no suspicious people walking or running in or near the vicinity. The actual office in question was in a back hallway; as we got closer, we could hear the alarm sounding, so— with weapons drawn—we made our approach. The actual suite door had been propped open, so we easily gained access; once in, we noticed the door to the room where the night's receipts are kept had been forcibly opened. In addition, the room appeared to be in disarray, and a sledge hammer was located on the floor, but we could not tell if anything was missing. We continued to check the area, but we found nothing had to have been tampered with. There were no suspects either.

Once we had secured the area, we cordoned it off and started to make phone calls. The first call was to the business manager. He stated they had not put the proceeds into the safe, and that approximately $25,000 had been left out in the open. The second call was to the investigative lieutenant to bring in investigators to process the area. Once the first investigator arrived on the scene, I assisted in taking pictures of the entire area and collecting/logging evidence. The evidence included the sledge hammer, fingerprints, and a pair of gloves found at the scene. In the meantime, Office Cameron began investigating means of possible *exit. The only unsecured area was the gate to the construction site, which was adjacent to the building housing the concessions business office. It was documented that the gate had been secured when it was checked earlier in the evening. That area was also processed as the possible exit/entry point.*

The investigation will continue later, but I needed to write a report nonetheless. When possible, I try to plan so that I don't leave report writing until the end of the day. Regardless of timing, though, I do follow a few basic tenets. An effective police report should be clear, concise, and complete. Similar to a newspaper story, it should answer the questions of who, what, when, where, why, and how. All information must be factual (nothing speculative or editorial in nature), and nothing can be left out (fill in blanks with NA, rather than nothing). In addition, it's important to print legibly and to ask another person to proofread. It's best to ask someone not involved in the case because an uninvolved reader will help you fill in the gaps.

Paperwork to be completed at this time includes original report, as well as the alarm drop and evidence forms.

Looking Back

Analyze Lieutenant Colonel Rose's writing process. One of her writing rituals is not to delay report writing until the end of the day; why do you think she does this? Do you think it saves time in the long run? Also, how would you describe her planning, drafting, revising, and polishing? Do they sound like separate or overlapping steps?

Looking Back

At what point does Lieutenant Colonel Rose establish probable cause? Throughout the investigation, is her conduct and procedure professional and leadership oriented? How does this allow her to lead by example?

Snapshot #3:
The Police Report for an Alarm Drop

At 0300 hours, Officer Cameron and I were dispatched to the Business Office for an alarm drop. Officer Cameron approached from the north side, and I approached from the east side. Neither of us saw nor heard any activity on the campus nor near the Business Office. Once we were inside the building, we could hear the alarm sounding. With our weapons drawn, we checked the area as we approached the Business Office. The suite door to the office had been propped open with a wooden wedge. As we searched the inside of the suite, we noticed the Business Office door had been damaged and was sitting open. The room was in disarray. Papers and chairs were scattered and drawers sitting open. A sledge hammer was sitting on the floor just inside the door. We continued to check the entire area and nothing else was found to have been tampered with. We found no signs of the suspect(s).

While Officer Cameron was securing the area, I made a phone call to Business Manager Neil Thomas. Thomas had said that the night's proceeds had not been put into the safe, and that the money had been placed on the table. He estimated that there was approximately $20,000 in cash. I then called the investigative lieutenant to have an investigator brought in to process the area. The investigator, Pete Harper, arrived at 0415 hours. I assisted him with processing the area and maintaining security of the area until it could be released. See Harper's attached report on the evidence collected and photographs taken.

While I was at the scene, Officer Cameron went to investigate means to a possible exit. The only unsecured area that he found was the gate to the construction area adjacent to the south side of the building. It was documented on my log sheet earlier in the evening that this gate was secured when I made a routine check. This area was also processed as a possible entry/exit point. See Harper's attached report for the evidence collected and photographs taken. Also see Cameron's report on his activities.

Looking Back

Analyze Lieutenant Colonel Rose's police report in terms of probable cause, officer conduct, and the five genre features:

- First-Person Perspective
- Objective Stance
- Accurate & Highly Specific Content
- Chronological Order
- Correct Format

Looking Back

Analyze Lieutenant Colonel Rose's police report in terms of the following items:

- Ethos/Leading by Example
- Paragraph Boundaries
- FCAs 1-10
- Concise Sentences

Chapter Review

Police reports are the most common documents written in the field of law enforcement, and they are, arguably, the most important document too.

Police reports must be written both effectively and efficiently. They provide an archived record of an investigation, one which lasts long after human memory fails. If a report is completed incorrectly or inaccurately, the investigative work is, at best, seriously compromised and, at worst, rendered null and void.

Police reports are a specific genre with six genre features: first-person perspective, objective stance, accurate & highly specific content, chronological order, multiple audiences, and correct format. These six genre features help the writer to establish *ethos*, that quality in a person that inspires confidence and trust.

There is a process for writing police reports, which may vary one police officer to another. Regardless, there is a strong relationship between the sequence of events during an investigation and the corresponding police report.

Police reports are linked to leadership. Good reports reflect positively on the report officer, promote PR, and allow the reporting officer to lead by example.

For Discussion

1. What are the names and ranks of the police officers in the three snapshots? Compare their background information and current positions.
2. What is the crime classification for each of the investigations?
3. How efficient are the three police officers in writing reports? What strategies do they use to streamline their writing processes? How does care early or in the middle of the writing process save time later?
4. Does each police report establish probable cause? Does each report document the responding officer's procedure and professionalism?
5. What are the six genre features of police reports? Are they present in each of the police reports?
6. Name the five multiple audiences. How do you think each kind of audience would respond to the individual police reports?
7. How do the police reports help each police officer establish ethos? Do the reports provide evidence of high standards in report writing? If yes, how will these high standards help the police officers lead by example?

TEST YOURSELF

Captain William K. Stewart of the New Philadelphia Police Department provided these practices exercises.

Practice Exercise 6.1

Read the scenario and then evaluate the corresponding police report. Explain if it demonstrates the six genre features: first-person perspective, objective stance, accurate & highly specific content, chronological order, multiple audience, and correct format.

You have been dispatched to 1340 Main Street to handle a complaint called in by Zoey Smith. The dispatcher has advised you that this is a domestic dispute going on between a male and a female, and that she can hear only yelling and screaming. You respond to the call and make contact with Zoey. You are the first officer on the scene, but other officers arrive within a few seconds. Zoey is visibly upset and crying uncontrollably. You notice that she has a red mark on the left side of her face that appears to resemble a handprint. She keeps telling you that her boyfriend, David Bell, is drunk and that he slapped her across the face for no reason. David is sitting in a recliner in the living room with an open beer on the table next to him. You hear him tell the other officers, "Yeah, I slapped the bitch. She wouldn't get me a beer when I told her to." Zoey tells you that she does not want David to go to jail, but she does want you to make him leave for the night. David informs you that he and Zoey are not married, but he did move in two weeks ago.

Police Report
DATE

Investigating Officer: Officer C. Polka

Victim: Zoey Smith (123-45-6789), 1340 Main Street, New Philadelphia, OH 44663, (330) 339-0101

Suspect: David Bell (987-65-4321), 1340 Main Street, New Philadelphia, OH 44663, (330) 339-0101

Initial Involvement
On January 1, 1999, the NPDP received a call from Zoey Smith of 340 Main Street. She advised of a domestic dispute involving her live-in boyfriend David Bell.

Investigation

I responded to the call and, with the other officers, made contact with the victim, Zoey Smith. She said that she and her boyfriend, David, had been arguing earlier, and that the argument escalated to a point that David slapped her across the face. Zoey did have red marks on her left cheek, but she said that she did not to pursue charges. She did submit a written statement but refused to sign the Domestic Violence Form.

While talking to Zoey, I overheard David tell the other officers that he had slapped Zoey because she would get him a beer. David was placed under arrest, transported to the police station, and advised of his Miranda Rights. At that point, he advised that he wanted to speak with an attorny prior to making any statement. He was booked in the New Philadelphia Jail and is currently being held, pending an appearance in court.

Practice Exercise 6.2

Re-visit the scenario in Practice Exercise 6.1 and write your own police report.

Practice Exercise 6.3

Read the following scenario and then write a corresponding police report.

You are dispatched to the K-Mart store on Bluebell Drive for a juvenile shoplifter. Upon arrival, you meet with the Loss Prevention officers at K-Mart. The employees report to you that they observed a juvenile take several items from the shelves and place them in his book bag. When this juvenile exited the store, a Loss Prevention officer stopped him. Upon returning to their offices, employees discovered items not only from K-Mart but also from Wal-Mart.

The juvenile's name is David L. Smith, and his address is 1234 Dyer Road, Sherrodsville, OH. He is 17 YOA and a student at Conotton Valley High School. The total dollar amounts from the K-Mart and Wal-Mart items are, respectively, $339.00 and $165.00. David advises that he lives with his father—David Smith, senior—and that he does not know where his mother is.

Practice Exercise 6.4

Read the following scenario and then write the corresponding police report.

You are dispatched to Ame's Department Store to investigate a shoplifting incident. Upon arrival, you meet with Jim Collins, a Loss Prevention officer. Jim advises that he observed a female remove clothing from the rack and then place the clothing into a large bag that she already had in her cart. This female then exited the store where Jim stopped her.

MyCompLab—Optional Exercises and Activities

As the homepage shows, MyCompLab is divided into three sections: Grammar, Writing, and Research. Under Writing, please do the following:

- Click Writing Process exercises and read Introduction to Prewriting, Planning, Drafting, Revising, and Finishing. Write a one-paragraph response to each introduction, indicating how the concepts are applicable to report writing.
- Click Writing Process exercises and gloss the various links under Pre-writing, Planning, Drafting, Revising, and Finishing. Which strategies correlate to those described in the snapshots of Under Sheriff Vinson, Deputy Chassé, and Lieutenant Colonial Rose? Be prepared to defend your response in small groups, class discussions, or written form, as your instructor requests.
- Click Exchange and Peer Review Help. Read all of the links under Peer Review Help to learn about the peer review process; then select two or three classmates to conduct a peer review of your responses to Practice Set 6.2, 6.3, and/or 6.4.

PART THREE

ADMINISTRATIVE DOCUMENTS: LEADING WITH THE WRITTEN WORD

Though the police report is arguably the most common and important document in the field of law enforcement, it is not the only type, especially as police officers are promoted to ranked positions. Like professionals in other fields and industries, as police officers are promoted, their writing responsibilities increase, becoming progressively more administrative and potentially more complex. To clarify, consider the wide range of administrative documents listed in the following table.

Common Administrative Documents

Year-End Reports	Commendations	Updates
Traffic Citations	Warnings	Schedules
Applications	Training Protocols	General Orders
Procedures	Internal Investigations	Policies
Grant Applications	Press Releases	Field Notes
Equipment Requests	Summaries	Feasibility Analyses
Letters	Regulations	Reprimands
Announcements	Thank-You Letters	Presentations
Flow Charts	Directives	Requests
Uniform Requirements	Speeches	Progress Reports
Memos	Rebuttals	Surveys
Recommendations	Cover Letters	Invitations
Counseling Letters	Reminders	Nominations
Minutes	Mission Statements	Agendas
Directories	Alerts	Guidelines
Newsletters	Advertisements	Course Descriptions
Cost Breakdowns	Personnel Evaluations	Goals

Though not exhaustive, this list showcases over fifty administrative documents, the types of documents that ranked police officers and their counterparts in other fields and industries are often called to write. Should a police officers be prepared to write at least this broad a range of administrative documents? The answer is that it depends on the police officer and his/her department. In large departments, ranked police officers tend to hold highly specialized positions, and their writing repertoires—in other words, the range and types of documents that they write—reflect their specializations. Try to imagine, for example, the administrative documents required of a police officer with a specialized position in field training, internal investigations, or youth services. As one might guess, police officers working in specialized positions write a lot; however, they tend to write fewer types of documents than their counterparts in small departments. In other words, their writing repertoires are smaller. In contrast, police officers in small departments are required to play multiple roles and, not surprisingly, their writing repertoires reflect that range. To clarify, try to imagine the administrative documents a police officer in a small department might write on any given day, week, or month. How would these administrative documents differ from those of a police officer with a highly specialized position?

Note: In many departments, police officers are identified as such outstanding writers that they become a "ghost writer" (a person who writes anonymously for another person) for their superiors. Ghost writers exist in all fields; in police departments, however, the most common case is for a lieutenant or captain to write administrative documents for the police chief's signature.

Regardless of department size, designated responsibilities and, in turn, writing repertoires, police officers and even those in other professions will benefit from Part III of *The Blue Guide* because each of the three chapters showcases a key strategy designed to dramatically improve administrative documents. The strategies are leading with purpose (Chapter Seven), incorporating indented lists (Chapter Eight), and articulating reader benefits (Chapter Nine). To explain these strategies, each chapter showcases original versions of actual police documents followed by a proposed revised version illustrating the key strategy in question. After each pair of documents, a wrap-up section called "Reading between the Lines" provides commentary comparing the two versions and explaining how the revised version would help better achieve the police officer's leadership goals.

CHAPTER SEVEN

BEGINNING DOCUMENTS WITH PURPOSE

I feel that my personal writing strengths are rooted in a strong educational background . . . one should always be looking for continuous ways to improve.

Sergeant John Paul Allsopp
Boardman Police Department
Boardman, Ohio

Leadership Objectives

- To learn how to begin documents with purpose; to see the leadership value in doing so.
- To render entire documents more direct and "to the point," thereby increasing professional self image, audience understanding and departmental productivity.

Assess Yourself

Collect ten recent documents, and read them carefully. While reading, be aware of the sequence of events that prompted you to write, but pay even greater attention to your primary purpose in writing. Ask yourself these questions:

- What is the Big Picture of each document? What is your purpose in writing and who is the audience. What leadership initiative did you hope to accomplish in writing? Having read each document, how do I want audience members to act?
- Where in each document is the articulated purpose? Underline the purpose. Is the purpose strategically positioned in each document or inadvertently buried?
- Does a pattern exist in your writing? Do you tend to lead with purpose or bury it? How much space do you allot to background information?

Most police officers have a tendency to organize documents in chronological order. This tendency probably stems from years of writing police reports, which are narratives (1) beginning with a dispatch call, (2) continuing with investigative details, and (3) ending with the current state of affairs. As every officer knows, the purpose of a police report is to document objectively a sequence of events, so chronological order is perfectly suited for the task.

This organization pattern, however, is not necessarily suited for all written communication. Though an interesting story or sequence of events is ultimately behind every administrative document, the document, itself, is not a narrative. Without fail, administrative police documents are either an informative or persuasive effort designed to implement some type or combination of leadership initiatives, and so the organizational pattern should stem not from the writer's memory of sequenced events, but from the audience members' needs.

What happens when police officers automatically revert to chronological order in their administrative documents? First, they typically provide too much background information, often allotting far more space for background information than for even their leadership initiative(s), and this approach wastes time for all concerned parties: both the writer and the reader. Even more importantly, it ensures that readers won't learn the writer's articulated purpose until the middle or even the very end of the document. In other words, the writer tends to inadvertently *bury purpose*.

To clarify, consider the following document written by Sergeant Brandon Lacy of the Warren County Sheriff's Office:

Writing Sample 7.1A

DATE

TO: Captain Miller
FR: Sgt. Lacy
RE: Use of Other Agencies' K-9s

Just a note to advise Command Staff members of our use of Hamilton County's K-9 and West Chester's K-9. On Saturday, 10/8/01, Deerfield units responded to the Summit Apartments ref. an armed robbery that just occurred. The suspects had a firearm and a Taser and robbed four subjects of $3000.00 cash and took all of their cell phones and tore the phone out of the wall. It was believed that the subjects were still somewhere in the complex so HCSO's dog was called to assist in the search. Once he was on the scene, we determined that the suspects had fled in a vehicle, but we felt that the call may have been a drug deal gone bad. We were able to use the dog to search the apartment of the victim for drugs. None were found but Dispatch advised that while the reportee was on 911 they heard the victims talking about hiding items. We were able to leave the scene confident that there was no illegal narcotics in the apartment that would eventually end up on our streets.

The second K-9 call of the weekend was early Sunday morning when units were dispatched to Timber Raid Drive ref. a subject breaking into a car. Minutes later units were on the scene and set up a perimeter. West Chester's K-9 was called, and he arrived on the scene 10 minutes later. The dog tracked all the way up the street and stopped at Snider Road where it was determined that the suspect got into a car and sped away. Due to the K-9, we were able to determine that the suspect had, indeed, left the area and we could free up other units to aggressively patrol other neighborhood areas to prevent further thefts.

While taking the report Dep. Hounshell was outside with the reportee. He inquired why West Chester was in Deerfield Township. He was shocked to hear the Sheriff's Office did not have its own K-9 program.

Officer Botman with the WCPD stated that he does not mind responding to Warren County because he knows how much of an officer safety issue it is not to use K-9s in many situations. He once gain offered his assistance in forming our own K-9 program and stated that the benefits were enormous.

Every deputy at WCSO agrees that we need K-9 more than anything else. Please contact me, and I can provide the command staff of all the facts and figures of starting a K-9 program of our own that we all can be proud of.

Writing Sample 7.1B

DATE

TO: Captain Miller
FR: Sgt. Lacy
RE: Request for a K-9 Unit

On behalf of the deputies, I am writing to renew the suggestion that Warren County Sheriff's Office consider implementing its own K-9 program. As you know, I have gathered all of the facts and figures associated with K-9 programs, and Officer Botman of the WCPD is still interested in sharing his time and expertise if we move forward with such a plan.

My renewed suggestion stems from two recent WCSO investigations. As the attached reports and summaries below show, the investigations are still underway; however, in each case, borrowed K-9 units played key roles in assisting law enforcement officials do their jobs:

1. On 10/08/01, Deerfield units responded to the Summit Apartments ref an armed robbery. The suspects, who had a firearm and a Taser, had just robbed $3000 from four subjects, and they had stolen their cell phones and ripped the regular phones from the wall. We believed that the subjects were still in the complex, so HCSO's K-9 was called to assist. Once he arrived, we determined that the suspects had fled, but we felt that the call may have been a drug deal gone bad, so the K-9 unit searched the victims' apartment. No drugs were found, and so WCSO deputies knew they could confidently leave the crime scene and continue the investigation more efficiently than they would have otherwise.

2. On 10/09/01, Dispatch called units to Timber Raid Drive ref. a subject breaking into a car. Upon arrival, we called West Chester's K-9 to the scene, and he tracked all the way up the street until stopping at Snider Road where it was determined the suspect had gotten into a car and sped away. In this case, the K-9 unit's search indicated that units could safely leave the neighborhood and aggressively patrol other areas to prevent further thefts.

These recent cases and many other previous cases provide evidence that both HSCO and West Chester are happy to share their K-9 units with the WCSO.

Looking Back

Compare the Big Picture of Sergeant Lacy's proposal with Scenario #3 in Chapter One. What does Sergeant Lacy understand about the relationship between written communication and leadership that the captain in the scenario doesn't understand?

Looking Back

What FCAs are demonstrated in Writing Sample 7.1B?

An interesting story clearly exists behind Sergeant Lacy's request. As Writing Sample 7.1A and B make clear, the Warren County Sheriff's Office does not have a K-9 unit, and Sergeant Lacy believes it needs one. To that end, he has taken the leadership initiative to complete the necessary research regarding the relevant facts and figures. In addition, he has sought the advice of a WCPD colleague offering to share his time and expertise, a fact providing evidence of Sergeant Lacy's excellent PR skills. Further, Sergeant Lacy's document suggests he has collegial support for a K-9 unit and he has already made at least one previous request to Command Staff members. His renewed request stems from two recent investigations, both of them greatly enhanced with the use of borrowed K-9 units.

Of the two versions of Sergeant Lacy's document, Writing Sample 7.1B is stronger because it leads with purpose. Let's face the facts. Command Staff members already know that the WCSO borrowed K-9 units for the two investigations in question, so there is no need to "advise" them (as Sergeant Lacy's original version does) before renewing the suggestion as a side note at the end. Why not be straightforward? Why not be direct? Sergeant Lacy is clearly a police officer with a good vision. By voicing that vision from the outset of his document, he comes across as more confident and forthcoming, two characteristics associated with effective leadership.

Though Sergeant Lacy may not need to "advise" the command staff of the two recent events involving a borrowed K-9 unit, he is wise to document them in his proposal. After all, he is most likely addressing a multiple audience (See Chapter Five for a full discussion of multiple audiences), and some readers may not be familiar with the recent departmental history. Itemizing the two events in a numbered list is the ideal rhetorical choice (see Chapter Eight for a full discussion of indented lists). First of all, the numbered list improves the visual impact of the document, so Sergeant Lacy comes across as more professional. In short, the itemized list raises the image of both the writer and the WCSO. Second, the numbered list positively draws attention to itself. Readers' eyes will be drawn automatically to it, thereby giving the attention that both incidents deserve.

The purpose of Chapter Seven is to illustrate the importance of leading with purpose. To this end, the chapter showcases two versions of five different police documents, followed by a discussion that compares the two versions. In each version, the articulated purpose is bolded for demonstration purposes.

DOCUMENT #1: A COMMENDATION LETTER

Original Version of Document #1

DATE

Chief Dennis Hanwell
Medina Police Department
150 West Friendship Street
Medina, OH 44256

Dear Chief Hanwell:

The Montville Police Department recently investigated a robber/burglary/kidnapping case where a young woman was abducted from her bedroom and forced to drive to an ATM to withdraw money. The investigating officer, Rich Percy, contacted Officer Paul Rocco of the Medina Police Department to create a composite sketch of the suspect. Officer Rocco was very helpful and willing to assist in any way possible. He came to our office and met with the victim for approximately four hours in order to interview her and perform the sketch. The sketch was subsequently released to the public and was instrumental in enabling us to obtain two separate leads, which directly led to the arrest of the suspect, Richard Sweiger. The sketch turned out to be very similar to Sweiger's actual appearance.

Officer Rocco kept in contact with Officer Percy and myself in support of our investigation. **He is to be commended for his assistance and willing cooperation which lead to removing a felon from our streets.** This is yet another example of the high level of cooperation which exists between our departments to the mutual benefit of Montville Township and the City of Medina. I look forward to our continued cooperation.

Sincerely,

Derek Bauman
Acting Chief of Police

cc: Mayor Jane Leaver
         Officer Paul Rocco

Looking Back

Speculate about Acting Chief Bauman's planning activities for the commendation. How do you think it might differ from planning a police report or a year-end report?

Revised Version of Document #1

DATE

Chief Dennis Hanwell
Medina Police Department
150 West Friendship Street
Medina, OH 44256

Dear Chief Hanwell:

I am writing to commend Officer Paul Rocco of the Medina Police Department for his hard work during our recent investigation of a robbery/burglary/kidnapping case. Upon request, Officer Rocco came to our office and spent over four hours interviewing the victim and creating a composite sketch of the suspect. His hard work paid off. When the sketch was released to the public, it was instrumental in obtaining two separate leads, one of which led directly to the arrest of the suspect, Richard Sweiger. Thanks to Officer Rocco's expertise and professionalism, a felon is off the streets.

This is yet another example of the high level of cooperation between our departments to the mutual benefit of Montville Township and the City of Medina. I look forward to our continued cooperation.

Sincerely,

Derek Bauman
Acting Chief of Police

cc: Mayor Jane Leaver
        Officer Paul Rocco

Looking Back

Consider the following sentence: *Upon request, Officer Rocco came to our office and spent over four hours interviewing the victim and creating a composite sketch of the suspect.* This sentence demonstrates FCA #2 (comma after introductory element, FCA #5 (job titles), and FCA #6 (comma before conjunctions).

Discussion: Reading between the Lines

The purpose behind Document #1 is clear. Acting Chief Bauman is commending Officer Rocco for his professionalism and expertise in a recent investigation. In both versions, he documents the officer's positive behavior, promotes good will between two neighboring police departments, and publicizes the same to the mayor. These outstanding goals mark Acting Chief Bauman as a leadership-oriented person and a solid writer.

The most important differences between the two versions are the opening sentences and overall organizational pattern. In the original version, the writer uses chronological order, so he begins objectively in narrative fashion with the details of the case, the contact made by the investigating officer, and Officer Rocco's willingness to help. From there, he continues with Officer Rocco's interviewing and sketching processes, the two subsequent leads, the final arrest of a suspect, and Officer Rocco's follow-up as the investigation continues. As the bolded portion makes clear, the primary purpose in writing—commending Officer Rocco—is relegated to a single sentence located in the middle of the last paragraph, and the letter concludes shortly thereafter.

In contrast, the second version of Document #1 leads directly with purpose: *I am writing to commend Officer Paul Rocco of the Medina Police Department for his hard work during our recent investigation of a robbery/burglary/kidnapping case.* This approach accomplishes four goals. First and most importantly, it places even more positive emphasis on Officer Rocco, and so it helps to better achieve his leadership initiative. Second, it enhances Chief Bauman's professionalism. He comes across as more direct because his opening is clear, concise, and to the point. Third, the approach saves time for both the writer and the reader because fewer details regarding the investigation are necessary to include. Moreover, the details that are necessary are not cast as objective background information but function, instead, as evidence supporting the positive claims regarding Officer Rocco. Last, the approach greatly enhances the conclusion. In the first version, Chief Bauman addresses three totally different topics in the final paragraph; in the second version, he highlights only one: the continued cooperation between the two police departments. This rhetorical strategy places greater positive emphasis on the cooperation, and it helps Chief Bauman's final words appear more unified and cohesive.

DOCUMENT #2: GENERAL ORDER

Original Version of Document #2

DATE

TO: All Officers
FR: Captain Lantz
RE: Harman School

As you know, parents picking up and dropping off students at the elementary schools has always presented challenges for the parents, school staff, and for the Public Safety Department. As foul weather approaches, the congestion will only increase. The schools have asked us to help them by being more vigilant during morning drop-off and afternoon dismissal times.

Harmon School has advised their parents through weekly newsletters that they are not permitted to sit (stand) in their parked cars in the no-parking areas of Harman and Dixon. The principal told parents they are allowed to pull to the curb and to have their children immediately exit the car during drop-off times. During pick-up times, the parents have been told to park legally and walk to the school to meet their children. The principal is trying to free as many legal spaces around the school as possible by having her staff park in the lower parking lot.

Starting Tuesday, September 24 (no school on Monday), I would like to have an officer, as manpower allows, at Harman School during the mornings, 8 AM to 8:20 AM, and during dismissal, 3 PM to 3:20 PM, to issue parking tickets to violators. The principal said warnings are not getting the point across to the parents (the issuing of tickets is always at the officer's discretion and warnings are fine if you decide a warning is appropriate). We should hit this hard for the first week and then evaluate the results. I expect to receive many angry calls from parents, but I will deal with them and support your efforts.

Looking Back

Consider this sentence: The principal told parents they are allowed to pull to the curb and have their children immediately exit the car during drop-off times. Should the "p" in principal be capitalized?

Revised Version of Document #2

DATE

TO: All Officers
FR: Captain Lantz
RE: Harman School

Effective September 24, an officer will be stationed weekdays at Harman School from 8:00–8:20 AM and from 3:00–3:20 PM to ensure that parents follow policies for dropping off and picking up their children. Though issuing tickets is always the officer's discretion, the principal claims that warnings are not getting the point across to parents.

For your information, parents know via the school newsletter that they are not permitted to sit in/stand by their parked cars in the no-parking areas of Harman and Dixon. Instead, they must pull momentarily to the curb during drop-off times and have their children immediately exit the vehicle. During pick-up times, parents should park legally and then walk to the school to meet their children. With this in mind, teachers are parking in the lower level lot to free as many legal spaces around the school as possible.

As you might guess, the plan is to hit this hard for the first week and then evaluate results. I expect to receive many angry calls from parents, but I will deal with them and support your efforts.

Looking Back

Reread the final paragraph of Captain Lanz's memo. Then explain the rationale for the two commas.

Looking Back

Analyze the paragraph boundaries in Captain Lanz's memo. Is paragraph length appropriate? Does each paragraph have a topic sentence and supporting details?

Discussion: Reading between the Lines

Captain Lantz's general order responds to such a common problem that he could have written it for virtually any police department. At the local elementary school, parents tend to violate parking procedures during morning drop-off and afternoon pick-up times, and so the general order calls for more vigilant patrolling during those peak hours, especially for the first weeks of September. Captain Lantz is to be commended for working cooperatively with the local school district and for anticipating problems associated with this current plan. He sounds like a leader.

The original version of Captain Lantz's general order is organized chronologically. It begins with past parking problems in the schools and the principal's written request to parents that they follow parking procedures, including a summary of those procedures as they were explained to parents. It continues with the principal's request for police assistance and then ends with purpose: the general order.

In contrast, the revised version begins with purpose (the general order): *Effective September 24, an officer will be stationed weekdays at Harman School from 8:00–8:20 AM and from 3:00–3:20 PM to ensure that parents follow policies for dropping off and picking up their children.* As a result, audience members immediately know Captain Lantz's expectations and, in turn, the school newsletter/ parking procedures explanation is transformed from background detail to vital information necessary for police officers to fulfill their duties. In the process, the information is condensed, which saves time for both the writer and the reader. In addition, Captain Lantz comes across as more direct and to the point.

DOCUMENT #3: THANK-YOU LETTER

Original Version of Document #3

DATE

Mr. Robert Baggs
Regional Transit Authority
1240 West 6th Street
Cleveland, OH 44114

Dear Mr. Baggs:

On Tuesday, July 23, our SWAT team hosted a bus interdiction training class in conjunction with HSS International Training Inc. We were given the use of two RTA buses for this training and the expertise of your employee, Scott McKernan. This was a very successful day of training. Our SWAT team and several other area SWAT team officers were able to learn a lot about transit buses from Scott. He explained how the buses operate and how to safely stop them. Scott stayed with us for the day and was able to answer all the questions we had throughout the entire training. **I just wanted to take this opportunity to let you know much help Scott was and to ask you to pass along to Scott our gratitude.**

Sincerely,

Robert Glaettli, Sergeant
SWAT Commander
Richmond Heights Police Department

Revised Version of Document #3

DATE

Mr. Robert Baggs
Regional Transit Authority
1240 West 6th Street
Cleveland, OH 44114

Dear Mr. Baggs:

Please accept my thanks for assigning Scott McKernan to the training class on bus interdiction hosted by the RHPD on July 23. As you know, Scott spent the entire day with us. As a result, he had the time to show everyone how to operate and safely stop a transit bus, and he could answer all questions as the training progressed. Thanks to Scott's expertise, SWAT team officers from my department and several other areas learned a great deal.

As this letter explains, we had a very successful day of training, and I hope you will pass along our gratitude to Scott.

Sincerely,

Robert Glaettli, Sergeant
SWAT Commander
Richmond Heights Police Department

Looking Back

Explain the usage rules for the two commas found in this sentence: As a result, he had the time to show everyone how to operate and safely stop a transit bus, and he could answer all questions as the training progressed.

Looking Back

Revisit the discussion of multiple audiences found in Chapter Five. Do you think that this letter will be read by multiple audiences? If yes, name the various audience members.

Discussion: Reading between the Lines

Sergeant Glaettli is wise in writing this thank-you letter. In doing so, he does more than simply document Scott McKernan's outstanding work; he simultaneously promotes positive RHPD/RTA relationships and, equally important, future cooperative ventures. In short, this letter demonstrates Sergeant Glaettli's leadership orientation.

The original version begins like a police narrative, documenting the date and purpose of training session, then introducing Scott McKernan, and finally explaining what took place as a result of his expertise. These observations include one evaluative comment—*This was a very successful day of training*—but the overall purpose/tone appears factual and objective, just like a police report. It's only in the last line that Sergeant Glaettli's real purpose emerges: his thanks for Scott McKernan's time and expertise.

The opposite is true in the revised version. In this document, Sergeant Glaettli opens by immediately expressing thanks for Scott's time and expertise: *Please accept my thanks for assigning Scott McKernan to the training class on bus interdiction hosted by the RHPD on July 23.* As a result, the letter no longer "feels" like a police report. Instead of having an objective stance, it's collegial and good-will orientated, which is consistent with the purpose of a thank-you letter. Moreover, the new opening places even more positive emphasis on Scott McKernan's work, and so it helps to better achieve the articulated purpose. Last of all, Sergeant Glaettli comes across as more direct, concise, and purposeful.

Note: In March 2005, Robert Glaettli was promoted to the rank of lieutenant.

DOCUMENT #4: WARNING

Original Version of Document #4

DATE

TO: All Officers
FR: W.L. Bretscher
RE: Cell Phone Usage

The first memo I put out a while back was to inform everyone that we had new cell phones and how we could use them and for what purposes we could use them. We did a nice job of following those guidelines, and I thank you for that.

During the past couple of months, we have encountered several large phone bills with these phones. Yes, you are paying for your personal calls, but a major problem has surfaced.

During the early part of the month, we are using up our allotted minutes and we then are having to pay a premium of any minutes over our base service. Also by eating up the monthly minutes we do not have any left for times that we really need them. Just for your knowledge, the November bill was over $200.00. In looking at the calls made and received on these phones, we have to make some changes. There is no need to call car to car, make numerous calls out to friends, receive calls from friends, cell to cell calls, or to call the dispatcher when we are as close to the building or a pay phone as we are. You can still call home if there is some type of problem that would require you to do from the cell.

Thank you for your understanding, and I look forward to not having to remove the phones from the cars, or putting mandated restrictions on them.

Revised Version of Document #4

DATE

TO: All Officers
FR: W.L. Bretscher
RE: Cell Phone Usage

I'm writing with potentially bad news. Unless department-wide changes take place, it may become necessary to remove the new cell phones from cars or to place mandated restrictions upon usage.

For your knowledge, the November bill was over $200, and there have been several other large phone bills in recent months. Yes, you are all paying for your personal calls; however, a serious and surprising pattern has emerged. We are collectively using up our allotted minutes in the early part of the month, and so the department ends up paying a premium for all minutes over our base service. To help avoid implementing a change in cell phone usage, please limit your usage. Emergency phone calls are fine, but please refrain from making/receiving unnecessary personal calls or from calling officers car to car. In addition, there is no reason to use a cell phone for calling dispatch.

As you recall, the first memo I wrote regarding the new cell phones outlined usage guidelines, and we did a nice job of following them. I thank you for that and encourage everyone to return to our previous cell phone practices.

Looking Back

Reconsider the following sentence: For your knowledge, the November bill was over $200, and there have been several other large phone bills in recent months.

Now answer these questions:

- What are the rules behind the two commas?
- Why is "$200" written as a digit and not a number?

Discussion: Reading between the Lines

The story behind Lieutenant Bretscher's memo is clear. His department recently initiated its first cell phone plan, one that has proven far more expensive then any city official or police officer could have anticipated. Though patrol officers naturally pay for their personal calls, these calls nonetheless "eat up" the department's allotted minutes, so the officers' personal calls, combined with calls for non-emergency police business, result in the department consistently exceeding its call plan and, in turn, accruing surcharges of over $200 for even valid business calls. Lieutenant Bretscher, then, has no choice but to address this issue.

In the original version of the memo, Lieutenant Bretscher's leadership purposes are strong and clear. He needs to warn his officers—with a fair and even hand—that cell phone usage must change immediately or the department will be forced either to ban cell phones or to create mandated restrictions. By putting this warning in writing (as opposed to announcing it at roll call), Lieutenant Bretscher demonstrates leadership orientation and rhetorical savvy. The memo formalizes the warning, so officers are more likely to take it seriously. Moreover, Lieutenant Bretscher knows that the memo functions as part of a paper trail in two ways: the memo documents for superiors that HE is doing his job, and it provides the necessary documentation, in case cell phone usage doesn't change and the department decides to take action.

Though the original version has great merit, the revised version is stronger because it leads with purpose. As a result, officers know immediately why Lieutenant Bretscher is writing and why: *Unless department-wide changes take place, it may become necessary to remove the new cell phones from cars or to place mandated restrictions upon usage.* By articulating purpose, Lieutenant Bretscher enhances his self-image because he comes across as being direct and pro-active: he is a leader who has assessed and is in control of the situation. After the purpose is articulated, the middle paragraph provides officers with a useful, fair-minded, and team-oriented explanation behind the warning, and then the new conclusion (which was cast as background information in the introduction of the original version) provides a positive endpoint.

Looking Back

Compare Lieutenant's leadership strategy with that of the captain in Scenario #5 found in Chapter One. Which leader do you believe is more successful and how good writing influence your opinion?

DOCUMENT #5: PROPOSAL

Original Version of Document #5

DATE

TO: Ken McFarland
FR: Ken Colburn
RE: Debbie Gardner's Survive Institute

I called Debbie Gardner on January 26, after receiving information from Chief Dickey. She conducts two- to three-hour seminars on surviving personal attacks, maintaining personal space and verbally asserting oneself. Debbie Gardner is a very dynamic person, conveying sincerity and optimism. She is a former Hamilton County Deputy Sheriff and is married to a Cincinnati police sergeant. The cost of her program is $1500. This is not a hands-on training session, but a lecture and demonstration.

I called Captain Hafer of Springdale Police Department for a reference. Springdale sponsored a Debbie Gardner program for their citizens and had to turn away over two hundred residents. They are co-sponsoring another program on February 22. Captain Hafer was very positive about the program and said residents, officers, and administrators were all impressed. They will be sponsoring more programs, due to the numerous inquiries they have received.

I feel that this program would be helpful for all of our employees and spouses, as well as school employees and spouses. I talked to Dr. Charles Wiedenmann on January 27. My proposal is for the City of Fairfield to pay for the program and for Fairfield City Schools to provide the high school auditorium for the program. Dr. Wiedenmann is receptive to this idea and suggested that if this approved, we could coordinate with Monica Mitter and Debbie Gardner to arrange a date. This would be an evening program, attended on a voluntary basis.

While this would be a benefit to our employees, we may want to consider future programs for our residents. Please call me if you have any questions. More information is available at surviveinstitute.com.

Revised Version of Document #5

DATE

TO: Ken McFarland
FR: Ken Colburn
RE: Debbie Gardner's Survive Institute

I am writing to propose the City of Fairfield and the Fairfield City Schools sponsor Debbie Gardner of Survive Institute to conduct a two- to three-hour lecture/demonstration regarding surviving personal attacks, maintaining personal space, and verbally asserting oneself. The workshop fee is $1500, and Dr. Charles Wiedenmann is receptive. If my proposal is accepted, he suggested that we coordinate with Monica Mitter and Debbie Gardner to arrange an evening session to be held in the high school auditorium. Attendance for this workshop would be voluntary and limited to city/school employees and their spouses, but possible future workshops could be open to the general public.

As Chief Dickey may have told you, Debbie Gardner is a dynamic speaker, conveying sincerity and optimism. She is a former Hamilton County deputy sheriff and a spouse to a Cincinnati police sergeant. Her recent Springdale Police Department workshop was apparently so successful that two hundred residents were turned away. According to Captain Hafer of the SPD, residents, officers, and administrators alike were all impressed, and plans are currently underway for future workshops, the next one already scheduled for February 22.

If you have questions or concerns regarding this proposal, please feel free to contact me or to visit the website: www.surviveinstitute.com.

Looking Back

Reread this document with capitalization in mind. Next, explain why the writer has chosen to capitalize the following:

> Chief Dickey
> Captain Hafer
> Fairfield City Schools
> Survive Institute

Discussion: Reading between the Lines

Lieutenant Ken Colburn's proposal provides concrete evidence of leadership skills. He has learned of an outstanding workshop designed to promote personal safety, and he believes that both city and school staff members, as well as their families, would benefit from attending it. To that end, he writes a proposal that includes a funding request for $1500 to cover the cost of the workshop and positive references from another police department. He also wisely describes relevant information about the workshop leader, which renders his proposal even more persuasive.

The original version of the proposal is organized in chronological order. Lieutenant Colburn starts at the beginning, documenting that he called the workshop leader and what he learned about her credentials, workshop fees, and workshop procedures. Next, he explains that he checked for references; in particular, he spoke with a captain at the Springdale Police Department and learned that a similar workshop was well received. Last, Lieutenant Colburn pitches his idea: that a workshop be conducted for city and school staff members, as well as their families. In addition, he notes that he has spoken with a school official who is receptive to the idea. In keeping with chronological order, Lieutenant Colburn closes by looking into the future in the hope that other similar workshops may one day be available for residents.

The revised version takes a different approach. Most importantly, it leads with the proposal idea: *I am writing to propose the City of Fairfield and the Fairfield City Schools sponsor Debbie Gardner of Survive Institute to conduct a two- to three-hour lecture/demonstration regarding surviving personal attacks, maintaining personal space, and verbally asserting oneself.* By leading with purpose, Lieutenant Colburn accomplishes two goals. First, he comes across as an even stronger leader because his message and tone are "direct and to the point." Second, he increases reader comprehension because the purpose is immediately set for audience members. After articulating purpose, Lieutenant Colburn continues with crucial facts for readers, including the cost and administrative support of the workshop, as well as workshop procedures and participants. In the second paragraph, he provides further support for the workshop by invoking his chief, who has exceptionally good things to say about the workshop leader. This information functioned as background information in the original version; in the second version, it provides further evidence for the worth of Lieutenant Colburn's proposal, making it even more persuasive to readers. It's true that the second version of the proposal has the same purpose as the first; however, the second version is more effective because it increases Lieutenant Colburn's professional image and is more reader focused.

Chapter Review

Police officers are trained to write police reports, which are organized chronologically. Though chronological order is the logical organizational pattern for police reports, it is not necessarily suited for the vast array of administrative documents that ranked police officers must write.

When police officers lead with purpose, their documents are more direct and "to the point." This strategy saves time for both the writer and the reader, and it ensures that readers are more likely to understand the writer's purpose and act accordingly.

For Discussion

1. Here are five purposes in writing: to motivate, to update, to reprimand, to alert, and to inform. Name ten more, being as specific as possible.
2. Imagine a specific type of administrative document for the fifteen purposes listed in Question #1.
3. Why does leading with purpose make documents seem more direct and leadership oriented?
4. If background information is important, how can you include it but still lead with purpose?
5. Can you think of a police document that should not lead with purpose? If yes, what would it be?
6. Collect ten documents. Read them carefully and then underline the articulated purpose. Is purpose articulated in the beginning, middle, or ending of the document? Does the purpose appear to be carefully placed or inadvertently buried? Why?
7. How is leading with purpose connected to leadership?

TEST YOURSELF

Practice Set 7.1

Read the document written by Sergeant Matthew Brown of the Centerville Police Department and then answer the questions following it.

DATE

TO: Lieutenant B. Robertson
FR: Sergeant M. Brown
RE: Annual Evaluation of Officer B. Bradshaw

I have had the opportunity to work with and supervise Officer Bradshaw for five months, and I have reviewed his previous evaluations. Officer Bradshaw is always neat and clean in appearance and prepared for duty prior to the beginning of his shift. He maintains excellent physical shape by working out regularly. Officer Bradshaw accepts direction and responsibility for his actions.

Officer Bradshaw usually met his self-initiated goals in conjunction with the number of days worked each month. On August 11, he received a letter of thanks for a citizen regarding a possible burglary in progress call on Laura Avenue.

On October 18, a CIR was initiated as Officer Bradshaw failed to locate a marijuana pipe that was left underneath the backseat of his cruiser from a previous shift. He was counseled on the importance of checking the cruiser for contraband at the beginning and end of each shift.

Officer Bradshaw used zero days of sick leave during the evaluation period.

Overall, Officer Bradshaw is a good employee and an asset to this department. I recommend he receive a merit pay increase.

Questions

1. What is the Big Picture of this administrative document? What is the purpose, audience, writer/reader relationship, and format? What prompted the writer to write in the first place? What do you think was the outcome?
2. Where is the purpose articulated in the document? How would the document change if it led with purpose?
3. What other changes would you recommend for a revised version? Why?
4. How does this document provide evidence of good leadership?

Practice Set 7.2

Read the document written by Lieutenant Kurt Byrd of the Cincinnati Police Department and then answer the questions following it.

DATE

TO: All Units
FR: Lieutenant Kurt D. Byrd
RE: NCCJ Walk as One/Freedom Run

The National Conference for Community and Justice (NCCJ) will be holding its annual Walk-a-Thon, the Walk as One/Freedom Run, on October 12. The Walk as One is the NCCJ's largest national fundraiser, and the Greater Cincinnati Walk is the most successful in the country. Annually, approximately 6,000 walkers participate in the Walk as One/Freedom Run and Greater Cincinnati's sixth annual Walk as One raised over $280,000.

NCCJ works with the Cincinnati Police Department on many worthwhile projects, including the Annual Police Youth "Live In," an annual five-day summer camp that provides inner-city youth and police officers the chance to live, work, and play together so that they can break down barriers and build relationships. Also, the NCCJ was instrumental in obtaining private funding for the department's newly created quarterly newsletter, "The Blue Wave," and assisted with its creation and publication.

The police chief has committed the department's participation in this event and is requesting personnel to join this worthwhile effort. All personnel interested in the Walk as One/Freedom Run should contact a team captain (see attached list) for the appropriate registration forms or for additional information.

Questions

1. What is the Big Picture of this administrative document? What is the purpose, audience, writer/reader relationship, and format? What prompted the writer to write in the first place? What do you think was the outcome?
2. Where is the purpose articulated in the document? How would the document change if it led with purpose?
3. What other changes would you recommend for a revised version? Why?
4. How does this document provide evidence of good leadership?

Practice Set 7.3

Read the document written by Sergeant Belinda Brooks of the Lake County Sheriff's Office and then answer the questions following it.

DATE

TO: Officer Peter Bonstone
FR: Sergeant Belinda Brooks
RE: Recent Behavior

The purpose of this mail message is to address your behavior during this rotation. Allow me to refresh your memory on the definition of general conduct, Policy and Procedure #0210: *Any employee shall be courteous to the public, shall be tactful, shall control his temper and exercise patience and discretion, not only with the public, but with co-workers. He shall not engage in argumentative discussions, shall not use coarse, violent, profane, or insolent language or gestures and shall not express prejudice concerning race, religion, politics, national origin, or similar personal characteristics.* Based upon observations by this officer, your behavior of late has violated several provisions of this policy.

As a supervisor, it is my responsibility to ensure that standard operating procedures are adhered to. When an employee displays a continual abuse of procedures, the need to address these actions falls upon the supervisor.

While I recognize that each employee handles stress levels in different ways, your chosen method of handling stress is not acceptable. I have observed a pattern: once a call is disconnected or radio transmission is completed, comments and/or name calling of citizens and officers has become a manner of routine for you. The continual name calling of officers is disrespectful and will not be tolerated. The continual comments about officers, citizens, and calls, in general, have proven to be annoying and disruptive to your co-workers. With the continual addition of new employees, this type of behavior is in direct opposition of what we present to new employees as expected and accepted behavior.

Be advised this documentation will serve as a counseling session. Should the need to re-address this area occur in the future, disciplinary levels will be initiated.

Should you wish to discuss any area of the contents of this documentation, it is expected that you will address your concerns with Lieutenant Greene or me.

Questions

1. What is the Big Picture of this administrative document? What is the purpose, audience, writer/reader relationship, and format? What prompted the writer to write in the first place? What do you think was the outcome?
2. Where is the purpose articulated in the document? How would the document change if it led with purpose?
3. What other changes would you recommend for a revised version? Why?
4. How does this document provide evidence of good leadership?

Practice Set 7.4

Create an administrative document triggered by the case scenarios listed below. Before writing, try to create a Big Picture for each scenario. After writing, check to ensure that each document leads with articulated purpose.

- Scenario #1: A large police department is in need of an additional juvenile officer. Write a letter to your shift supervisor suggesting that the department request this position.
- Scenario #2: A small town city council is requesting nominations for Citizen of the Year. Write a nomination for an outstanding colleague.
- Scenario #3: The chief wants to create a student mentor program for your police department. Draft a set of guidelines for this program and be sure to include a cover memo.
- Scenario #4: A local business owner could prevent being a crime victim with a few simple operational changes. Write a letter that outlines these changes.
- Scenario #5: After learning of several MIP arrests involving local teenagers, the school superintendent has asked the police department to conduct an alcohol awareness workshop at two high schools. Write a response accepting the invitation and proposing a workshop agenda.

MyCompLab—Optional Exercises and Activities

Under Writing, click Model Documents and then select and read these professional communication documents: recommendation memo, letter, instructions, proposal, and report.

- What is the purpose of each document? Who is the audience? Under what circumstances is the writer writing? In other words, what is the Big Picture?
- Is the purpose implied or articulated? If the purpose is articulated, note its placement within the document. Does the document lead or end with purpose, or is the purpose located somewhere in the middle?
- If the document doesn't lead with purpose, can you explain why the author might have made this choice? Would the document be stronger if it led with purpose? Why?

CHAPTER EIGHT

INCORPORATING INDENTED LISTS

An organization is no better than the people who work within it. To that end, I attempt to represent myself and others professionally in writing.

Assistant Chief Richard Amweg
The Ohio State University Department of Public Safety
Columbus, Ohio

Leadership Objectives

- To learn how to incorporate indented lists in police documents; to see the leadership value in doing so.
- To enhance visual impact of documents, thereby increasing the professional image of both the law enforcement leader and his/her police department.
- To understand that an indented list improves reading comprehension, so that leadership initiatives are more easily understood and efficiently implemented.

Assess Yourself

Collect ten recent documents and read them carefully. Then ask yourself the following questions:

- What is the Big Picture of each document? What is the purpose and who is the audience? What leadership initiative did you hope to accomplish in writing? Having read each document, what did you want audience members to do?
- Do any of the documents include an indented list? If yes, what does the indented list achieve? If not, why not?
- For each document, circle the section that includes the most important content. Could the circled sections be reformatted as an indented list? Why? Why not?

Most police officers intuitively know to incorporate indented lists in departmental policy, by-law, and procedure documents. However, an indented list—either bulleted or numbered—is also an excellent strategy for virtually any administrative document. The reason is simple. An indented list provides additional "white space" and "textual variation" within a document, so it enhances visual impact and, in turn, increases the professional image of both the police officer and his/her department. Equally important, an indented list enhances reading comprehension because it sets off key information within the larger document. Because the information is set off, readers' eyes are automatically drawn to it. In other words, police officers who incorporate indented guide readers toward both better understanding and faster implementation of leadership goals.

Looking Back

Chapter One identifies "re-imagining a document with enhanced visual impact" as a good revision strategy. With practice, however, a police officer might find it just as easy to incorporate an indented list during the drafting.

Looking Back

Reread this sentence: Because the information is set off, readers' eyes are automatically drawn to it. Explain the apostrophe rule, focusing especially on apostrophe placement and how it relates to the plural noun (readers).

To better understand the value of indented lists, consider the two versions of the following memo written by an anonymous lieutenant in an Ohio police department:

Writing Sample 8.1A

DATE

TO: All Night Detectives
FR: Lieutenant XYZ

RE: Case Tracking System

Gentlemen,

Lieutenant Biernstein and I have been working on a new system to track the status on the cases detectives are working on in the major crime units. Each detective has been assigned a working case file drawer where the open cases for each detective will be kept. We will no longer be taking case files home, unless a separate copy has been made for this purpose. Regardless of whether a copy has been made or not, a case file for each case will be maintained here at the department in the assigned drawer. The need for this is simple; at times, victims call in to check on the status of their case or suspects are located on open cases during hours other than our regular scheduled shift. The supervisors from other shifts need to have access to all active cases for each detective so in the event that immediate follow up is needed on a case, they can access the case file and see what direction the case has been heading in and assist with the case. I will also be starting a monthly case review program with each detective. The monthly review is not to find out whether you have been working or doing investigations correctly. I know we are all busy and the cases just keep coming in. Everyone is working and doing a good job with their investigations. By having the monthly review of cases, my goal is to gain a better understanding of what is going on in the open cases for each detective and give any guidance, suggestions, or assistance with the case. I hope to make this change in the way cases are managed, tracked, and reviewed as smooth as possible so any suggestion once it has been implemented to make it run smoother will be appreciated.

Looking Back

The lieutenant's original salutation is the word, "Gentlemen," the assumption being that each night detective is a man. Memo format aside (see Appendix A), what is the advantage and disadvantage in using this salutation? To answer this question, please revisit FCA #8.

Writing Sample 8.1B

DATE
TO: All Night Detectives
FR: Lieutenant XYZ
RE: Case Tracking System

Lieutenant Biernstein and I have been working on a new system to track the status of the cases detectives are working on in the major crime units. Here are the two major components:

- "Open Case" File Drawers. Each detective has been assigned a file drawer for all his/her open cases. This file draw should continuously house all relevant working materials for each open case (take home no originals!). The need for this file drawer system is clear; it provides immediate access of all open cases to supervisors from other shifts, in case (a) a victim calls for an update or (b) a development occurs.
- Monthly Case Reviews. Each detective will meet with me on a monthly basis to review all open cases. My goal here is not related to performance evaluation. Instead, my purpose is to gain a better understanding of each open case in order to provide any guidance or support.

I hope these two components will improve the managing, tracking, and reviewing of all open cases. Once the system has been in place for a month or two, please evaluate its effectiveness from your perspective and share all suggestions for improvement with Lt. Biernstein or me. I would greatly appreciate your input.

What is the difference between Writing Sample 8.1A and B? A close reading reveals that the overall message and basic content order are essentially the same. Both memos begin with purpose, continue with two proposed procedural changes, and conclude with a feedback request. Equally important, both documents demonstrate the lieutenant's strong leadership intentions. As a law enforcement leader, he evaluated the Big Picture of his department and recognized a flaw in the then-current tracking system of the open cases in the major crime units. His proposed procedural change offers a potential resolution to this flaw, and he is confident enough to request further evaluation and improvement suggestions after an initial test period. Best of all, the lieutenant explains the procedural change and its rationale in writing, which formals the procedure and grants it permanence.

The primary difference between the two versions is the indented list, with each bullet identifying one of the two procedural changes. This list accomplishes three goals. First and most obviously, the bulleted list enhances visual impact. Though the message is essentially the same, it looks more professional formatted as a list (instead of one overly long paragraph). Second, the bulleted list actually encourages the lieutenant to be more "clear, concise, and to the point" because bulleted items tend to be shorter than full-length paragraphs. Last, it renders the memo more "reader focused" because the readers' attention is drawn to the most important information, in this case the two procedural changes. As a result, the document is more accessible and audience members are more likely to not only read, but also understand, the message. In other words, an indented list increases the Power of the Pen, so leadership goals are more likely to be implemented efficiently.

The purpose of Chapter Eight is to illustrate the value of incorporating indented lists. To this end, the chapter showcases two versions of five different police documents, followed by a discussing that compares the two versions.

Note: As this chapter shows, law enforcement leaders enhance visual impact when they incorporate indented lists in their written communication. For a list of other visual impact strategies, see Appendix C.

DOCUMENT #1: A "SUSPICIOUS INCIDENT" ALERT

Original Version of Document #1

DATE

TO: Morning Shift

FR: David Gehringer

RE: Suspicious Incident at Addison Elementary School

I took a complaint from a John Siebert this evening regarding an incident at Addison Elementary School. He advised that his daughter, Alice, who is in the first grade (Mrs. Lender's class), brought home a letter which was in her "mailbox" at school. When they opened it, they found it said I want to kill you. It was signed by April.

The children are seated four to a table. Alice is seated with April Baxter, Mark Apter, and another unknown student. Alice and April have been "on and off" friends. They are currently not friends. Alice recently told April she does not wish to be friends because April gets in trouble. Alice believes that Mark received an envelope, as well. However, we have not heard anything from him or his parents.

We need to have a unit get started checking on this before school starts, I believe, at 8:50. The children do not ride a bus together. I've left the letter and envelope in your mailbox.

Mr. Siebert works out of town area but advised he can return to town, if you need him. His wife, Paula, can be reached at the house. I told him we would contact him and let him know what was going on.

Looking Back

Locate Sergeant Gehringer's purpose in the original version of his memo, and then find it in the revised version. Which placement better serves his purpose?

Looking Back

Sergeant Gehringer addresses his memo to the Morning Shift. Are there multiple audience members (see Chapter Five).

Revised Version of Document #1

DATE

TO: Morning Shift

FR: David Gehringer

RE: Suspicious Incident at Addison Elementary School

I took a complaint from a John Siebert this evening regarding an incident at Addison School. He advised that his daughter, Alice, brought home a letter, which had been placed in her "mailbox" at school. When they opened the envelope at home, Mr. and Mrs. Siebert found a letter saying, "I want to kill you," and it was signed "April."

We need to have a unit start checking on this complaint before school starts at 8:50. To that end, here is the pertinent background information:

- The letter and envelope are in your mailbox.
- Alice is a first grader in Mrs. Lender's class.
- The children are seated four to a table; at Abby's table are Alice Siebert, April Baxter, Mark Apter, and another unknown student.
- Alice and April are "on and off" friends, and they are currently not friends because, according to Mr. Siebert, Alice told April recently that she didn't want to be friends because April gets in trouble.
- Alice believes that Mark also received an envelope, but we have not heard from him or his parents.

I told Mr. and Mrs. Siebert that we would provide an update. Mr. Siebert works out of town but will return to town if you need him, and Mrs. Siebert can be reached at home.

Looking Back

Notice the quotation marks in this sentence: When they opened the envelope at home, Mr. and Mrs. Siebert found a letter saying, "I want to kill you," and it was signed "April." Are the quotation marks necessary? What is the rule for punctuating direct quotes? Why do you suppose Sergeant Gehringer decided to quote the letter?

Discussion: Reading between the Lines

Sergeant Gehringer's fine leadership intentions are clear in both the original and revised versions of his memo. A local first grader has allegedly received a threatening note from a classmate, and he wants immediate action. In response, he has quickly gathered the necessary information and provided it for the appropriate personnel. For such a potentially serious matter, the sergeant knows there is no time to waste.

Though the content is virtually the same in both versions, the revised version better serves Sergeant Gehringer. Most obviously, the purpose is articulated early in the second version (See Chapter Seven for a full discussion on this topic). After one paragraph of crucial background information, he states the purpose upfront: *We need to have a unit start checking on this complaint before school starts at 8:50 AM.* In addition and most relevant here, the crucial information is summarized for readers using five bullet points. The bullet points accomplish three goals. First, they enhance visual impact, so Sergeant Gehringer comes across as a more professional and sophisticated writer. Second, the bullets demonstrate Sergeant's Gehringer's proactive stance; he has not only gathered, but also analyzed, the crucial information for readers' benefit. Third, readers can see "at a glance" the crucial information, which is more efficient than reading a paragraph or two.

Note: Notice that the bullet points are written in the same basic manner. Each point is comprised of a single complete sentence. When writing bullet points, it's important that each one follow the same basic pattern.

DOCUMENT #2: GUIDELINES FOR REQUESTING VACATION TIME

Original Version of Document #2

DATE

TO: All Patrol Personnel

FR: Tom Bishop, Captain

RE: Vacation Scheduling

**The deadline for submitting your vacation request will be
Sunday, February 24**

As most of you are aware, some of the senior officers gain an additional week of vacation this year, bringing the number of weeks they must schedule up to three weeks. This will make it even more important to get your request in by the deadline.

Scheduling vacation requests will be by seniority. Any vacation request received after the deadline will be scheduled on a "first come, first served" basis. All vacation requests will be scheduled with consideration of regular operations in mind. Except for extenuating circumstances, there will be no vacation request granted, if they would cause a disruption of regular levels of manpower (determined by command staff) on any particular shift.

If you have questions or clarification is needed on this matter, please see me.

Looking Back

What is the Big Picture of Document #2. Does the document achieve any of the following?

- Build self-image.
- Enhance public relationships.
- Promote policies and procedures.
- Increase *esprit de corps*.

Looking Back

In the original version of Document #2, does Captain Bishop lead with purpose?

Revised Version of Document #2

DATE

TO: All Patrol Personnel

FR: Tom Bishop, Captain

RE: Scheduling Deadline/Procedures for Vacation Time

I am writing to inform you that the deadline for submitting a vacation request will be Sunday, February 24. This deadline is especially important because, as you may know, several senior officers gain an additional week of vacation this year, bringing their total vacation time up to three weeks.

On February 25, the chief will schedule vacation time using these procedures:

- Requests will be ranked based upon officer seniority.
- All requests will be considered in light of regular operations. No requests will be granted if command shift determines it will compromise regular staffing levels.
- Late requests (after February 24) will be considered on a "first come, first served" basis.

If you have questions or need clarification on this matter, please see me.

Looking Back

Do the bullet points in the revised version of Document #2 highlight the key information? Are the bullet points listed consistently?

Looking Back

Reconsider the subject line: Scheduling Deadline/Procedures for Vacation Tim. Is the subject line correctly capitalized?

Looking Back

Explain the rule for each comma listed in Document #2.

Discussion: Reading between the Lines

Vacation time is a top personnel issue in any organization, so Captain Bishop shows proactive leadership by documenting procedures in writing—especially in this case, with several senior officers eligible for three weeks of vacation instead of two.

In both versions of the memo, Captain Bishop wisely leads with articulated purpose (announcing the deadline for submitting a vacation request) and then continues with the procedures involved. These procedures include ranking requests by seniority before the deadline, ranking requests on a "first come/first serve' basis after the deadline, and considering all requests in light of daily operations. In the original version, the procedures are listed in a paragraph; in the revised version, they are formatted in a bulleted list.

The bulleted list is stronger. It allows readers to see "at a glance" the crucial information that they need to understand departmental procedures for requesting vacation time. It's easy to imagine officers "checking off" each of the bulleted items quickly and with complete understanding. In short, the bulleted list is more concise and accessible than a paragraph. Equally important, the bulleted list enhances visual impact; with a bulleted list, the memo looks more professional, and so Captain Bishop's professional image is also enhanced. It's a win-win situation for everyone involved.

Looking Back

Captain Bishop's document deals with personnel matters. Do you suppose that Under Sheriff Vinson or Lieutenant Colonel Rose (see Chapter Six) write similar documents, given that their job responsibilities includes personnel matters?

DOCUMENT #3: AN INVITATION TO JOIN A COMMITTEE

Original Version of Document #3

DATE

TO: All West Carrollton Employees

FR: Robert Hensley, West Carrollton Police Department

RE: An Invitation to Join the Recommendation/Recognition Committee

One of my new assignments is to chair the Recommendation/Recognition Committee. The committee was formed to open lines of communication among departmental employees; to provide a process by which departmental employees can contribute to changes in the operations of the department, and to offer suggestions on new programs or improvements to existing programs.

It also provides a uniform means of recognizing actions or acts performed by members of the police department which are either outstanding or beyond that which is normally expected.

I am looking for volunteers form the entire police department to make up the committee. I need one officer from each shift, one clerk/dispatcher, and one civilian employee.

If you are interested, please put a note in my mailbox by August 8. If you have questions, please see me.

Looking Back

Analyze Writing Sample 9.14A by answering the following questions:

- What is the Big Picture of this document? What is its purpose?
- What do you suppose was Sergeant Hensley's writing process? How much time do you think he spent planning, drafting, revising, and editing?
- How many sentences are in each paragraph? Which paragraphs could be logically combined?

Revised Version of Document #3

DATE

TO: All West Carollton Employees

FR: Robert Hensley, West Carrollton Police Department

RE: An Invitation to Join the Recommendation/Recognition Committee

As the new chair of the Recommendation/Recognition Committee, I am writing to invite you to become a committee member and help hardworking colleagues earn the recognition they deserve. In particular, I need five volunteers:

- Three Shift Representatives (one from each shift)
- One Clerk/Dispatcher
- One Civilian Employee

As you may know, the committee was formed for three reasons: (1) to open communication lines among departmental employees, (2) to provide a process by which departmental employees can contribute to changes in the operations of the department, and (3) to offer suggestions on new programs or improvements to existing programs. Most importantly, the committee provides a uniform means of recognizing actions performed by police department members that are outstanding, that is, "above and beyond" the call of duty.

If you are interested in serving on this important committee, please see me with questions or put a note in my mailbox by August 8.

Revised Version II of Document #3

DATE

TO: All West Carrollton Employees

FR: Robert Hensley, West Carrollton Police Department

RE: An Invitation to Join the Recommendation/Recognition Committee

As new chair of the Recommendation/Recognition Committee, I am writing to invite you to become a committee member and help hardworking colleagues earn the recognition they deserve. In particular, I need five volunteers: three shift representatives (one from each shift), one clerk/dispatcher, and one civilian employee.

As you may know, the committee was formed for three reasons:

1. Open communication lines among departmental employees.
2. Offer a process by which departmental employees can contribute to changes in the operations of the department.
3. Offer suggestions on new programs or improvements to existing programs.
4. Provide a uniform means of recognizing outstanding actions performed by police department members that went "above and beyond" the call of duty. This is the most important purpose of all.

If you are interested in serving on this important committee, please see me with questions and/or put a note in my mailbox by August 8.

Looking Back

Chapter Five explains that police reports are written in first person and with an objective stance. Sergeant Hensley's document is written in first person, but it doesn't have an objective stance? What sentences keep it from "sounding" like a police report? Is this a good or bad feature of the memo?

Discussion: Reading between the Lines

Sergeant Hensley is a leader in the true sense of the word. He has volunteered to chair a city committee and, in this role, sends a respectful and welcoming invitation to his colleagues, encouraging them to consider joining the committee. Each version of the memo clarifies the committee's mission and the number/kind of committee members needed. However, an important difference separates the original and revised versions: an indented list. The original version is comprised of four paragraphs and does not include a list, while the two revised versions do, though the list in each version showcases different information.

In the first revised version, Sergeant Hensley leads with purpose and then bullets the number and kind of volunteers that he needs: *three shift representatives, one clerk/dispatcher, and one civilian employee.* In the second revised version, he leads with purpose, quickly identifies the number and kind of volunteers he needs, and then bullets the mission of the committee: *open communication lines among departmental employees, provide a process by which employees can contribute to changes in operations, offer suggestions for new/existing programs.* Of the two approaches, which is better? Does it make more sense to showcase the necessary volunteers or the committee's mission? The answer is that it depends. It depends on what content Sergeant Hensley wants to emphasize.

Regardless, the bulleted list in both revised versions is an excellent rhetorical strategy. First, it enhances visual impact because a bulleted list looks better on the page than a series of four short paragraphs (see Chapter Four for a fuller discussion of paragraph boundaries). Second, a bulleted list provides a more positive image of Sergeant Hensley. He looks more professional and leadership-oriented—which he clearly is! Last, the bulleted list promotes reading comprehension because the key information is accessible for readers so they quickly peruse it and act accordingly.

DOCUMENT #4: YEAR-END REPORT

Original Version of Document #4

DATE

TO: Lt. Brad Conner

FR: Sgt. Alan W. Carsey

RE: EZ+ Year-End Report

The Bowling Green Police Division EZ+ team officers continue to coordinate this program. The current members of the team are: Ptl. Grant Tansel, Ptl. Scot Becker, Ptl. Brian Crites, Ptl. Ray Baer, Ptl. Jason Broshious, Ptl. Terry Davis, Ptl. Robin Short, and Ptl. Justin Shite.

The EZ+ program had 524 members in the 2001–02 school year, or 92% of the student enrolllment at the Bowling Green Junior High School. Of the 524 students, 224 were instructed in the EZ+ curriculum in Mrs. Teri Geer's health classes. Ptl. Crites, R. Baer, and Short assisted Ptl. Tansel in teaching the curriculum.

The Police Division sponsored six EZ+ dances and two school activities in which Police Division officers and school volunteers mentored students.

The program continues to positively affect the youth of Bowling Green.

Revised Version of Document #4

DATE

TO: Lt. Brad Conner
FR: Sgt. Alan W. Carsey
RE: EZ+ Year-End Report

During the school year, the Bowling Green Police Division EZ+ Team has continued to positively affect area youth. In fact, the program enrolls 524 students, or 92% of the student body at Bowling Green Junior High School.

The program sponsored nine curricular or extra-curricular activities:

- EZ+ Curriculum in Mrs. Teri Geer's Health Classes
- EZ+ School Dances (6)
- EZ+ School Activities (2)

Police Division members are Ptl. Grant Tansel, Ptl. Scot Becker, Ptl. Brian Crites, Ptl. Ray Baer, Ptl. Jason Broshious, Ptl. Terry Davis, Ptl. Robin Short, and Ptl. Justin Shite.

Looking Back

The second sentence demonstrates FCA #1: Numbers. Can you explain why "524" and "92%" are written as numerical digits, not words?

Looking Back

What planning activities would be necessary to write a year-end report? What drafting, revising, and polishing activities would also be necessary to complete for submitting the report?
    Who are the audience members for a year-end report?

Looking Back

Revisit the case studies in Chapter Six. Of the three police leaders, who indicated that writing year-end reports was a job responsibility? Speculate why it might be required of all police leaders?

Discussion: Reading between the Lines

Year-end reports are factual documents, and Sergeant Carsey's report is a textbook example. By writing it, he provides Lieutenant Connor (and all future multiple audience members) with the names of EZ+ patrol officers, the number/percentage of participating students, and activity highlights.

The original version of Document #4 is not organized chronologically. In other words, Sergeant Carsey does not provide a month-by-month or quarter-by-quarter description of the EZ+ Program but instead wisely provides a general overview of the year. This overview, however, is stronger in the revised version, first of all, because of the differences in the introductions and conclusions. In the original version, Sergeant Carsey leads with what appears to be background information—patrol officers' names and student participation rates—and he concludes with his overarching point: *The program continues to positively affect the youth of Bowling Green.* This sentence functions as a useful summary or capstone for the original report, but it makes an even stronger opening, as the revised version demonstrates.

By leading with the program's success, Sergeant Carsey's revised document takes on a persuasive edge. Student participation rate, for example, is no longer background information but, instead, concrete evidence of excellent departmental work. The most important information, however, is highlighted in the bulleted list. It identifies three different kinds of curricular/extra-curricular items, including the EZ+ curriculum in a health class, six dances, and two school activities. Readers can see "at a glance" this information, and so they are more likely to be impressed by it. It's important to note, too, that the visual impact of the report is enhanced by the bulleted list. That's because an indented list of any kind provides additional white space and textual variation from the standard paragraph.

The revised version of Sergeant Carsey's report still achieves its primary goal, which is to document police work. In addition to documenting the program, however, Sergeant Carsey also markets it. In other words, he is no longer merely informing readers; he is guiding them and, in process, better able to showcase more accurately the excellent work of the EZ+ Program.

DOCUMENT #5: REQUEST OF COMMUNITY MEMBERS

Original Version of Document #5

DATE

Dear Resident,

Your cooperation is needed in helping reduce the amount of burglaries in Springfield Township. We have instituted the Operation Identification Program to help you help us. Operation Identification is a program designed to both help prevent burglaries and to help track down any stolen merchandise that may be taken in a burglary.

So many times in the past, we have taken burglary reports from residents who did not know the make, model, or serial number of their valuables. This makes it hard for us to recover their merchandise. So many items during our investigations, we come across merchandise we know to be stolen but are unable to identify the owners due to the fact owners failed to know serial numbers of their stolen valuables. When valuables are reported to the Police Department as stolen, we are able to put those items in a nationwide computer, providing we have the make and serial numbers of those items. If this is done correctly, then a police officer anywhere in the country can run suspected stolen items through the computer system and the computer will indicate that the items are stolen and where they are stolen from.

The subject found with the stolen items is then charged with receiving stolen property. They are immediately questioned and about how they received those items and sometimes this leads to the arrest of subjects responsible for the burglary and the possible recovery of additional stolen items.

The second benefit of Operation Identification is that it helps prevent burglaries. After you have shown the Police Department that you have copied down identifying features of your valuables, the Police Department provides you with a couple of door and window decals to display at your home that informs would be burglars that items of value in your home have been marked for identification purposes. The would-be burglar then knows that those valuables would be hard to keep or sell due to the fact that they can be traced back as stolen.

Please fill out the attached paperwork identifying your valuables. If your valuable does not have an identifying serial number, then engrave or scratch an identifying number on the item (the Police Department has engravers you can borrow for this purpose). Suggested numbers are the last four digits of your social security number. After filling out the paperwork, make two copies and keep them in separate locations, possibly one at your place of employment or with a trusted friend. The information on this paperwork is also information your insurance company would need in case of a theft.

Thank you in advance for your cooperation. Hopefully, we can work together to cut down the burglaries and keep burglars on the run.

Revised Version of Document #5

DATE

Dear Resident,

I am writing to request your cooperation in an innovative program designed to reduce or prevent the ill effects of township burglaries. **The program is called Operation Identification, and you can participate by following the directions regarding the attached paperwork:**

1. Itemize all valuables in your home, including both the make/serial number. For items without serial numbers, scratch or engrave any number, such as the last four digits of your social security number. The Police Department has an engraving tool for this purpose.
2. Make two copies of the itemized list, one copy for your home and one copy for a separate location, such as your workplace or a friend's home.
3. Take the completed paperwork to the Police Department and receive a free window/door decal that alerts would-be burglars that you are Operational Identification participant.

Why should township residents participate in this new program? Most importantly, if you are a victim of theft, you can report stolen items to the Police Department, and an officer will immediately enter the make/serial numbers into a nationwide computer system. This system has the capability of cross referencing the serial numbers of stolen and suspected stolen property across the country so that your valuables are more likely to be found and the thieves in question tracked and arrested. Residents might be surprised to learn how often theft victims right here in Springfield Township report stolen property but don't know the necessary make/serial numbers. They might also be surprised to learn how often police confiscate stolen goods that can't be returned because owners haven't reported make/serial numbers. Operation Identification seeks to resolve both of these serious problems.

There are two other important reasons to participate. First, if displayed properly, Operation Identification window/door decal may prevent thieves from burglarizing your home because they know stolen items can be more easily traced. Second, the paperwork required for the program is essential for insurance purposes.

Thank you in advance for your cooperation. Hopefully, we can work together to cut down the burglaries and keep burglars on the run.

Springfield Township
Garry Moneypenny, Captain

Discussion: Reading between the Lines

Captain Garry Moneypenny writes with the best of leadership intentions. He wants to help residents track stolen property and prevent burglaries from happening in the first place. There is no question that this leadership goal is consistent with his departmental mission statement and an overarching goal of the entire field of law enforcement. To that end, he requests residents' participation in Operation Identification because it provides an accessible system for documenting the make/serial numbers of their valuable possessions.

Though Captain Moneypenny leads the original version with an explicit participation request, readers don't learn how to participate until the very end of the document. In contrast, the revised version provides this information up front and in a numbered list so leadership intentions are more accessible and—even more importantly—likely to take place. More specifically, there are three steps: (1) Complete the itemized list, (2) Make the appropriate copies, and (3) Bring the paperwork to the Police Department. With this approach, the rationale for participating, which should logically follow the request, is cast not as background information that police officers have experienced but as concrete evidence for the audience members' point of view.

The difference is remarkable, and it accomplishes these goals. First, Captain Moneypenny comes across as an even more effective leader because his written communication is direct and to the point, and it has much stronger visual impact. Second, audience members' reading comprehension increases. They know immediately what Captain Moneypenny wants them to do and can see, in turn, how it would directly impact them (as opposed to how to might have helped other people in the past).

Looking Back

Take a close look at the "bullet openings" in Captain Moneypenny's letter. What do they have in common? Compare his openings with those found in the revised versions of Document #3.

Chapter Review

Indented lists enhance the visual impact of police documents, thereby increasing the professional image of both the police officer and his/her police department.

Indented lists increase reading comprehension so that leadership initiatives are more easily understood and implemented.

For Discussion

1. What is visual impact? Think for a moment about the average newspaper, and then name ten strategies that editors use to enhance the visual impact. Do the same for a popular magazine. Note: See Appendix C for more information about visual impact.
2. How does an indented list enhance visual impact?
3. Why does an indented list increase reading comprehension?
4. Are leadership initiatives more likely to be efficiently implemented when they are explained in an indented list? Why?
5. How does an indented list help law enforcement leaders write more concisely?
6. Would you prefer to incorporate an indented list during the drafting and revising stage of the composing process? Why?
7. What kind of content might work well for an indented list?
8. Collect ten recent documents that you have written and read them carefully. Would any of the documents be enhanced with an indented list? If so, explain why.

Practice Set 8.1

Read the document written by Lieutenant Kurt D. Byrd of the Cincinnati Police Department and then answer the questions following it.

DATE

TO: Lieutenant Howard L. Rahtz, Acting Police Academy Director
FR: Lieutenant Kurt D. Byrd, Public Information Office/Executive Officer
RE: Letter of Reference—Mr. Kyle Strunk

E911 Operator Kyle Strunk has requested that I write a letter of reference for him as he is in the recruiting process as a potential candidate for police recruit.

I had the pleasure of working with Kyle while he was a police cadet assigned to the Public Information Office (PIO). Kyle consistently represented the Police Department in a professional manner. As part of his daily duties, Kyle was expected to multi-task many issues relating to law enforcement. In addition, he was expected to deal with the members of the department, the Command Staff, and the media and public on a daily basis. He completed all of his assignments in an exemplary manner. Kyle continually kept a positive outlook in this assignment.

Kyle has had the opportunity to experience many facets of law enforcement due to his prior assignments in PIO and now his present assignment in the Police Communication section. These experiences have given him the opportunity to make an educated career choice.

Based upon my daily observations of Kyle while assigned to this office, I feel he possess many characteristics necessary to become a successful career police officer.

Questions

1. What is the Big Picture of this administrative document? What is the purpose, audience, writer/reader relationship, and format? What prompted the writer to write in the first place? What do you think was the outcome?
2. Would this document be enhanced with an indented list? If yes, what content should be part of the list and how would this change alter the document?
3. What other changes would you recommend for a revised version? Why?
4. How does this document provide evidence of good leadership?

Practice Set 8.2

Read the document written by Sergeant Gregory Petek of the North Ridgeville Police Department and then answer the questions following it.

DATE

TO: All Units
FR: Sergeant Petek
RE: Rule 4 Waiver Form

Attached is a copy of our new Rule 4 Waiver Form, which was adapted from the Lorain County Sheriff's Department. The new forms will be kept in the cabinet above the computer in the booking room.

If a prisoner is willing to waive the Rule 4 hearing, fill out this form and have him/her sign it. The arresting officer/transporting officer will sign it along with another witness. The entering agency receives the original signed form when a representative arrives to pick up the prisoner. Please make a copy of the form and staple it to the prisoner's booking sheet. If you have any question or problem, please let me know. Obviously, we do not run into this a lot, but this will hopefully save us some time and the hassle of transporting to the county.

Questions

1. What is the Big Picture of this administrative document? What is the purpose, audience, writer/reader relationship, and format? What prompted the writer to write in the first place? What do you think was the outcome?
2. Would this document be enhanced with an indented list? If yes, what content should be part of the list and how would this change alter the document?
3. What other changes would you recommend for a revised version? Why?
4. How does this document provide evidence of good leadership?

Practice Set 8.3

Read the document written by Sergeant Terrence Lowry of the Harrison Police Department and then answer the questions following it.

DATE

TO: Lieutenant S. Wilson
FR: Sergeant T. Lowry
RE: 90-Day Counseling—Officer Pinsey

Attached to this letter, you will find a copy of a 90-day counseling form given to Officer Pinsey. I counseled Officer Pinsey on two items of concern. In violating a failure to report for duty, concerning an off-duty basketball detail at the high school, Officer Pinsey felt he should stand by at the station to make sure there was enough road coverage. There were only two officers in uniform on the road.

I explained to Officer Pinsey that although I understood his concern, five officers were actually on duty at the time. Although three of the five officers were in soft clothes, Officer Petty and I were also working off-duty details and were in full uniform. Additionally, I stressed to him the importance of being to an assigned duty on time and understanding the chain of command. If he had a concern, he should have brought it to the attention of the shift OIC.

The other item, an argument between Officer Pinesey and Detective Sniderman, was also discussed. Officer Pinsey was advised that an argument between officers cannot be tolerated in the workshop. Officer Pinsey was advised of several options for handling future disagreements, including diffusing the situation, walking away, or asking for supervisory help. I stressed that getting into a shouting match is not an option.

Officer Pinsey has assured me that no animosity exists between Detective Sniderman and him. He feels he can learn a lot from Detective Sniderman and respects his capabilities as a law enforcement officer.

Questions

1. What is the Big Picture of this administrative document? What is the purpose, audience, writer/reader relationship, and format? What prompted the writer to write in the first place? What do you think was the outcome?
2. Would this document be enhanced with an indented list? If yes, what content should be part of the list and how would this change alter the document?
3. What other changes would you recommend for a revised version? Why?
4. How does this document provide evidence of good leadership?

Practice Set 8.4

Create an administrative document triggered by the case scenarios listed below and also found in Practice Set 8.4. Before writing, try to create a Big Picture for each scenario. After writing, check to ensure that each document leads with articulated purpose and includes a bulleted list.

- Scenario #1: A large police department is in need of an additional juvenile officer. Write a letter to your shift supervisor suggesting that the department request this position.
- Scenario #2: A small town city council is requesting nominations for Citizen of the Year. Write a nomination for an outstanding colleague.
- Scenario #3: The chief wants to create a student mentor program for your police department. Draft a set of guidelines for this program and be sure to include a cover memo.
- Scenario #4: A local business owner could prevent being a crime victim with a few simple operational changes. Write a letter that outlines these changes.
- Scenario #5: After learning of several MIP arrests involving local teenagers, the school superintendent has asked the police department to conduct an alcohol awareness workshop at two high schools. Write a response accepting the invitation and proposing a workshop agenda.

MyCompLab—Optional Exercises and Activities

Under Writing, click Model Documents and then select and read these professional communication documents: recommendation memo, letter, instructions, proposal, and report.

- What is the purpose of each document? Who is the audience? Under what circumstances is the writer writing? In other words, what is the Big Picture?
- Does the document contain an indented list? If yes, what information has been indented? What purpose is achieved by setting off this information?
- If the document doesn't contain an indented list, can you explain why the author might have made this choice? Would the document be stronger if it included an indented list? Why?

CHAPTER NINE

ARTICULATING READER BENEFITS

By communicating in writing with others, I feel that I am viewed as honest, open-minded, and informative. The morale of our unit has never been higher, and I would like to think that my style of supervising and communicating has something to do with it.

Sergeant André D. Douglas
Cleveland Police Department
Cleveland, Ohio

Leadership Objectives

- To understand what reader benefits are.
- To learn how to incorporate reader benefits in police documents; to see the leadership value in doing so.
- To render entire documents more reader focused and, thereby, promote audience buy in and, in turn, leadership initiatives.

Assess Yourself

Collect ten recent documents and read them carefully. Then ask yourself the following questions:

- What is the Big Picture of each document? What is the purpose, and who is the audience? What leadership initiative did you hope to accomplish in writing? Having read each document, how do I want audience members to act?
- Are reader benefits associated with each document? If yes, what are the benefits and are they implied or explicit in the document? In other words, are the benefits specifically stated or not?
- For each document, imagine a section devoted exclusively to reader benefits? Where would this section logically be placed, and what would the content be? How would it influence audience members' response?

Police departments are inherently hierarchical institution, operating under a strict chain of command. What the chief asks of the captains, lieutenants, and sergeants must be done; likewise, what the captains, lieutenants, and sergeants ask of patrol officers must also be done. Because of this "top down" institutional structure and culture, police officers have not traditionally recognized the value in articulating reader benefits in their administrative documents. They most likely assumed that audience members would comply with directives, regardless of whether they perceived reader benefits or not. However, police officers often send administrative documents up the chain of command or, in the case of external documents, outside of it. In both cases, articulating reader benefits is an important strategy in enhancing written communication and, in turn, achieving leadership goals and initiatives.

Even when police officers write down the chain of command, they may want or truly need "audience buy-in" to achieve their goals. After all, as Speed B. Lease points out in *Discover Your Conflict Management Style,* it's possible for leaders to compel others—that is, to use personal or professional authority to force others into following directives; however, the cost is often decreased morale, low motivation, and possibly even sabotage (12–17), none of which support the police leader.

According to Kitty O. Locker's *Business and Administrative Communication*, all professional writers should seriously consider articulating reader benefits:

> Reader benefits are benefits or advantages that the reader gets by using your services, buying your products, following your policies, or adopting your ideas. Reader benefits are important in both informative and persuasive messages. In informative messages, reader benefits give reasons to comply with the policies you announce and suggest that the policies are good ones. In persuasive messages, reader benefits give reasons to act and help overcome reader resistance . . . good reader benefits are adapted to the audience, are based on intrinsic rather than extrinsic advantages, are supported by clear logic and are explained in adequate detail . . . (69)

To clarify the importance of reader benefits, consider the following document written by Detective Sergeant David Ferrell of the South Russell Police Department:

Writing Sample 9.1A

DATE

TO: Chagrin Falls High School Parents and Students
RE: Underage Drinking and Student Safety

On May 15, Chagrin Falls High School will be hosting its senior prom, and the last day of school for seniors is May 14, with graduation taking place on June 6. Other local schools celebrate these events during the same time period.

I'm sure you are aware that students sometimes during these celebrations have the opportunity to consume alcohol. **In order to reduce the likelihood of a student injuring him/herself or someone else after consuming alcoholic beverages, our police department will be strictly enforcing alcohol violations.**

Enforcement will include compliance checks in conjunction with the Ohio Investigative Unit, bar checks, party checks, and more rigorous traffic enforcement. Any underage child caught with alcohol will be prosecuted. **The purpose of this letter is to keep our loved ones safe during this time of year.**

I am enclosing a brochure, "Parents Who Host—Lost the Most," which will give you valuable information about underage drinking and parties.

Please feel free to contact me if I can be of any assistance to you in an effort to keep these children from buying and drinking alcohol.

Sincerely,

Detective Sergeant David Ferrell
South Russell Police Department

Writing Sample 9.1B

DATE

TO: The Parents and Students of Chagrin Falls High School
RE: Underage Drinking and Student Safety

As you know, CFHS will host its senior prom on May 15, and the last day of school for seniors is May 14, with graduation on June 6. Other local schools will be celebrating these **events too. With these community events and student safety foremost in mind, the SRPD will work in the coming weeks with the Ohio Investigative Unit to increase alcohol violation enforcement, including more rigorous bar/party checks and traffic enforcement. Any underage child caught with alcohol will be prosecuted.**

I am enclosing a brochure, "Parents Who Host—Lose the Most," which provides valuable information about underage drinking and parties. **The purpose of this brochure, as well as the intent of this letter and the rationale for increased enforcement, is to keep our loved ones safe. Each spring across the country, literally dozens of teenagers are killed in alcohol-related accidents, and we can only imagine the devastation resulting from these senseless deaths. The children are gone from this earth forever, while their parents—along with siblings, grandparents, teachers, and friends—will mourn for the rest of their lives. As a community, we must do everything in our power to prevent such a terrible loss this year.**

Please feel free to contact me if I can be of any assistance as we work together to prevent CFHS teenagers from buying and drinking alcohol.

Sincerely,

Detective Sergeant David Ferrell
South Russell Police Department

As Writing Samples 9.1 A and B make clear, Detective Sergeant David Ferrell is a hero. Like hundreds of law enforcement personnel across the country, he is gearing up for the myriad spring celebrations taking place in rural communities, small towns, and major cities. Too often, these celebrations result in underage drinking and, in turn, senseless deaths. The purpose of the letter to the CFHS parents and students is noble and leadership oriented: Detective Sergeant Ferrell wants to help keep teenagers safe. To accomplish this goal, he explains plans for increased alcohol enforcement and provides an informational brochure.

The purpose is the same in both versions of the letter, but two key differences exist. The first difference is overall organization. Writing Sample 9.1A is a series of five relatively short paragraphs, and Writing Sample 9.1B combines related paragraphs for a total of three (see Chapter Four for a fuller discussion of paragraph boundaries). The more significant difference, however, is the emphasis on reader benefits. In 9.1A, Detective Sergeant Ferrell indicates that he is primarily interested in student safety, and any reader would agree. His subject line, for example, is "Underage Drinking and *Student Safety*," and he explicitly states in the third paragraph that the purpose of his letter is to "*keep our loved ones safe during this time of the year*." It's clear that this police officer cares about the wellbeing of children, just as his readers do. In 9.1B, that same level of caring and concern is clear, but then it's significantly extended as a result of the articulated reader benefits in the second paragraph. Here, the letter asks parents to consider the emotional devastation resulting from a child's alcohol-related death. Gory details of the accident scene are wisely omitted, but the letter does provide a painful reminder of how commonly teenagers are killed every spring, and any loving parent can't help but imagine the unspeakable horror of losing a child. Articulating reader benefits greatly enhances the effectiveness of Detective Sergeant Ferrel's letter.

The purpose of Chapter Nine is to illustrate the importance of articulating reader benefits. To this end, the chapter showcases two versions of five different administrative documents written by police leaders, and then it follows with a discussion comparing the two versions. In each version, reader benefits are bolded for demonstration purposes.

DOCUMENT #1: A PROPOSAL TO A SCHOOL SUPERINTENDENT

Original Version of Document #1

DATE

Dr. Sylvester Small, Superintendent
Akron Public Schools
70 North Broadway
Akron, OH 44308

Dear Dr. Small:

In light of the current climate in school buildings across the country, I would like to offer a suggestion as to how parents/guardians could be kept informed about the status of their school as it relates to early dismissals, closings, delays, and lockdowns. The Washington County, Maryland school district built an email distribution list that can be sent to any parent or guardian who subscribes to it with one click of the mouse. This distribution list request is on their website and was used during the sniper shootings to keep the parents in the area informed.

The emails would lessen the amount of calls made to the buildings and could even be used to disseminate important information, like reminders to vote for Issue 12. My last suggestion would be to add school closings and delays to the APS website for fast review as opposed to a crawl across the television screen or listening for Akron Public Schools on the radio.

Sincerely,

Lieutenant CA Brown
Commander
Community Relations/COPS

Looking Back

Is the punctuation correct in the first sentence of the second paragraph? Revisit FCA #6 to be sure.

Looking Back

Does this letter written to multiple audiences, even though solely one person is named in the salutation? How does the superintendent's high-ranking position influence Lieutenant Brown's writing process?

Revised Version of Document #1

DATE

Dr. Sylvester Small, Superintendent
Akron Public Schools
70 North Broadway
Akron, OH 44308

Dear Dr. Small:

In light of current technology and recent school tragedies across the country, I'm writing to propose two suggestions for increasing communication within the Akron community.

First, I propose that routine school closings, delays, and early dismissals be posted on the APS Webpage. **If approved, this suggestion would be easy for your district clerical staff to implement, and it would save time for individual school secretaries by reducing the onslaught of telephone calls they routinely receive from concerned parents. Most importantly, the postings would be good PR for the APS because there would be increased school-community communication than radio announcements and/or television crawls currently provide.**

Second and perhaps more importantly, I propose the APS consider building an email distribution list for parents/guardians. **If approved, the district could send emergency messages—with a one click of the mouse—to the entire school community.** You might be interested to know that email lists have been successfully piloted in a number of school districts, including Washington Country, Maryland. When the recent sniper shootings began, the list proved invaluable to school officials as they worked with law enforcement to inform the community of developing information. **My fervent hope, of course, is that Akron will never face such a school tragedy; however, I'm sure you agree that it is wise to be prepared. School tragedies aside, an APS distribution list would be an effective and efficient way of, for example, reminding parents to vote on school-related issues or to attend upcoming events at any of the area schools.**

It might be useful to discuss these two proposals in person, and so I'll call within the next week or so to set up a meeting.

Sincerely,

Lieutenant CA Brown
Commander
Community Relations/COPS

Discussion: Reading between the Lines

By writing to the school superintendent, Lieutenant Brown shows strong leadership initiative and a proactive stance. He knows that law enforcement personnel and local school officials are often called to work together as a team, so he wisely proposes that the superintendent consider building an email distribution list, in case the APS ever faces a school shooting. In addition, he proposes the possibility of posting routine closings and/or delays on the district Webpage, a good idea designed to enhance communication within the community. Moreover, it is clear in both versions of Lieutenant Brown's letter that he has the school district's best interest in mind.

In the first version, one sentence is devoted to reader benefits: T*he emails would lessen the amount of calls made to the buildings and could even be used to disseminate important information, like reminders to vote for Issue 12.* However, a strong implied reader benefit is clear when Lieutenant Brown invokes the school sniper shooting in Washington County, Maryland. Any superintendent would "connect the dots" and see the relevance.

Even so, the revised version better serves Lieutenant Brown. First, it leads with the less controversial suggestion—the idea of Webpage postings—and then fully "rounds out" the benefits for the APS, including easy implementation, time saved, and good PR. In the original version, this suggestion was offered in the conclusion. Second, the revised version introduces the more controversial suggestion—the creation of an email distribution list—and then describes successful pilot programs, *including the one in Washington County, Maryland.* The implication here is also clear, but it is extended this time with a follow-up statement: *My fervent hope, of course, is that Akron will never face such a school tragedy; however, I'm sure you agree that it is wise to be prepared.* The idea of being prepared, then, is an explicit reader benefit, one that any school superintendent would value (and share with local law enforcement leaders). Last, Lieutenant Brown "shifts gears" and suggests that an email distribution list would be a means of reminding community members of upcoming levies and school events—again playing to the values/needs of the superintendent.

DOCUMENT #2: A COUNSELING LETTER

Original Version of Document #2

DATE

TO: Officer Barbara Bender
FR: Sergeant Steve Farmer
RE: Counseling

This memo is in reference to our conversation today concerning correct documentation in your report writing.

In January, we discussed the paperwork associated with the Ari Alexander case. There were several omissions in the arrest packet, as well as concerns from the court clerk regarding the incorrect ORD numbers and the corresponding degrees of offense. Since this conversation, errors have continued. The paperwork for three recent investigations have been returned for several corrections. You have been an active member of the shift, which is appreciated; however, you are expected to take the time to be thorough in your documentation in order to prepare for the successful resolution of each case. At this time, I do not believe this is a training issue; however, if you believe that training would be beneficial, let me know and we will move in that direction.

PLEASE NOTE THAT THIS COUNSELING IS DESIGNED TO CORRECT THE PROBLEM AND NOT A DISCIPLINARY MEASURE, although disciplinary action could result from future actions.

Thank you for your attention.

Looking Back

The first line in Sergeant Farmer's memo suggests that it was written the day of the conversation. Why do you suppose he wrote so promptly? How does this approach support Lieutenant Colonel Rose's claims about making time for writing on a daily basis?

Looking Back

This counseling letter reprimands an officer for poor report writing skills. What seems to be the problem with the reports in question. Consider the ramifications of the officer's poor reports in light of Chapters Five and Six.

Revised Version of Document #2

DATE

TO: Officer Barbara Bender
FR: Sergeant Steve Farmer
RE: Counseling

This memo is in reference to our conversation today concerning correct documentation in your report writing.

As you know, we discussed the paperwork associated with the Ari Alexander case last January. At that time, we talked about several omissions in the arrest packet, as well as the court clerk's concerns regarding the incorrect ORD numbers and the corresponding degrees of offense. Since this conversation, errors have continued. The paperwork for three recent incidents has all been returned for several corrections, and this is completely unacceptable. You have been an active shift member, which is much appreciated; **however, you are expected—as a sworn officer of the Dublin Division of Police—to take the time to be thorough in your documentation. No matter how diligently and professionally you and your shift members investigate a case, it's all for nothing if you write an incorrect police report. In other words, a thorough report is your primary means of ensuring a successful case resolution. You learned this basic and time honored concept years ago during police academy.**

At this time, I do not believe these errors stem from a training issue; however, if you believe that training would be beneficial, let me know and we will move in that direction. If not, **please note that this counseling is designed to correct the problem and not function as a disciplinary measure**, although disciplinary action could result from future actions.

Thank you for your attention.

Looking Back

Do you believe that Sergeant Farmer's counseling letter will prompt positive change? Do you think it will increase esprit de corps, even for the officer in question? How does the memo provide evidence of Sergeant Farmer's ethos? Does he sound like a good leader?

Discussion: Reading between the Lines

Sergeant Farmer's counseling memo is a textbook example. As a shift sergeant, he is obligated to document officer misconduct, and Officer Bender's incomplete reports fall into this category. The purpose of his memo (and all counseling memos) is to help the officer correct his/her problem and, equally important, to begin the necessary paper trail, in case future infractions occur. For this reason, most counseling documents follow a certain pattern: neutral tone, specific information, and a warning of potential future disciplinary action. Sergeant Farmer is a good writer and a police leader, and so it's not surprising that his counseling memo follows this pattern.

Though overall purpose is identical in both versions, the revised counseling memo better serves Sergeant Farmer and the officer in the question. The major difference is the articulated reader benefit in the middle paragraph:

> *[Y]ou are expected—as a sworn officer of the Dublin Division of Police—to take the time to be thorough in your documentation. No matter how diligently and professionally you and your shift investigate a case, it's all for nothing if you write an incorrect police report. In other words, a thorough report is your primary means of ensuring a successful case resolution. You learned this basic and time honored concept years ago during police academy.*

This passage articulates two points that Officer Bender clearly knows but has apparently forgotten: First, she is a sworn officer of the law, a position requiring basic core values: integrity, honor, and teamwork. The phrase, sworn officer, is worth repeating in a counseling memo because it invokes the core values likely to promote positive change. Second, Officer Bender learned as a police cadet that an investigation is only as good as its report. If she takes her own investigative work seriously and values the work of her peers, then she needs to change her report writing. This reminder is worth repeating because it places the onus of the counseling where it properly belongs: on the officer in question. In other words, the reminder makes clear that the counseling session is designed to promote the officer's professionalism and career growth—both important reader benefits.

DOCUMENT #3: A PROCEDURAL UPDATE

Original Version of Document #3

DATE

TO: All Units
FR: Sergeant Demmitt
RE: Crash Scene Safety

Chief Fogle from the Marion Fire Department and two representatives from the Marion County Fire District were recently on post to discuss scene safety. They had a few issues regarding crash scenes and making the scene as safe as possible for both the victims and emergency personnel.

Their concern is when we allow traffic to continue moving past a scene while they are still conducting patient removal and/or treatment. Lieutenant Church and I explained our position and policy in protecting the scene while allowing traffic to continue, if at all possible. We explained that allowing traffic to back up is a hazard and if this can be avoided, we tend to keep traffic moving, which also decreases motorist frustration in having a road blocked. Chief Fogle understands our position and just wants us to be vigilant in taking care of the scene and protecting his units from vehicle traffic.

Remember to arrive on scene and first look for ways to keep the scene safe. If the fire/emergency squad has not arrived yet, look for a place they can park the trucks without blocking the whole road, if possible. While they're tending to the victims, watch the traffic. The traffic flow is **our** responsibility. It's easy to get tunnel vision and walk right out into traffic. We all know of the adrenaline rush when the lights and sirens are going, and it's the same for them, especially the volunteers. They forget about all the traffic that may be moving around them. Some of the volunteer departments are starting to not allow their units to direct traffic because of the liability. Our pictures and measurements will be there after they're done.

Every scene is different, so assess what is needed. Don't be afraid to talk with the firefighters. **See what they need; after all, they may be pulling you out of a car one day.**

Keeping the scene safe is a joint effort for both us and the emergency personnel on the scene. We don't want to do their job, so let's make sure we protect them. The motoring public tends to obey us more than the firefighters. After all, we issue the tickets.

Revised Version of Document #3

DATE

TO: All Units
FR: Sergeant Demmitt
RE: Crash Scene Safety

Chief Fogle from the Marion Fire Department and two representatives from the Marion County Fire District were recently on post to discuss scene safety. Their primary concern is that we allow traffic flow past a crash scene while they are still conducting patient removal and/or treatment. Lieutenant Church and I explained our position and policy in protecting the scene, indicating that traffic back ups are motorist hazards too, and so we keep traffic flowing, if at all possible. Chief Fogle understands our position, asking nonetheless that we be vigilant in taking care of the scene and protecting his units from vehicle traffic, and I hope you agree that his request is reasonable and fair-minded.

The meeting serves as a reminder to all that crash scene safety is a joint effort. For this reason, state troopers (perhaps more than any other police division) must work in cooperation with emergency personnel to protect and serve. As we all know, traffic flow is our responsibility, and the motoring public tends to obey us more than firefighters when it comes to traffic control. After all, we issue the tickets. **On the other hand, we don't want to do the work of emergency personnel, so let's do everything possible to ensure their safety at crash scenes. In particular, here are a few reminders:**

- Every scene is different, so begin by assessing what is needed. While assessing, don't hesitate to talk with the firefighters to learn their needs are. **Put yourself in their shoes and remember: they might one day be pulling you (or a loved one) out of a car.**
- **Your top priority is crash scene safety. If the fire/emergency squads have not arrived, locate a place where they can safely park,** if possible without blocking the whole road.
- **After fire/emergency squads arrive and begin their work, do yours: watch the traffic.** We all know the adrenaline rush caused by lights and sirens, and it's the same for them, especially volunteers. Like us, they just want to do their jobs and may forget all about the traffic and walk right into it.
- Remember that our pictures and measurements will be there for further investigative work long after fire/emergency squads have left the crash scene.

Thank you for your consideration. Please let me know if you have further suggestions or questions.

Discussion: Reading between the Lines

Sergeant Demmitt is an effective police officer who understands the importance of teamwork. His memo demonstrates that he is a team player in the Ohio State Highway Patrol, protective of his troopers and mindful of their rights and responsibilities in crash scene safety. On the other hand, he recognizes and greatly values the teamwork required of state troopers and the fire/emergency squads. He knows that each group must do its job, working together toward a common goal.

This value in teamwork is clear in both versions of Sergeant Demmitt's memo, and he uses it to his advantage. More specifically, Sergeant Demmitt knows that his troopers value teamwork as a concept as much as he does, so he capitalizes on this shared value to drive home his point: to complete their own important work, state troopers must help fire/emergency squads do theirs. Interestingly, the content is virtually the same in both memos; the difference is organization and slant.

In the first version, Sergeant Demmitt spends the first two paragraphs (nearly the first half of the memo) documenting his meeting with Lieutenant Church, Chief Fogle, and the two other fire representatives, and he uses the remaining space to outline safety procedure. There is no single section devoted to reader benefits associated with teamwork; instead Sergeant Demmitt incorporates words, phrases or sentences "here and there" stressing the importance of teamwork. In contrast, the second version begins with a condensed overview of the meeting, and then it moves immediately and *explicitly to section devoted to reader benefits associated with team work: The meeting serves as a reminder to all that crash scene safety is a joint effort. For this reason, state troopers (perhaps more than any other police division) must work in cooperation with emergency personnel to protect and serve.* The rest of this paragraph supports the teamwork concept and then even the procedural reminders are couched within a teamwork framework, with each bullet emphasizing the importance of working cooperatively and productively with fire/emergency personnel.

Looking Back

Chapter Eight indicates that bullet points are sometimes more effective than full paragraphs. Do you believe that Sergeant Demmitt's message is clearer with bullet points found in the revised version? Why ?

DOCUMENT #4: AN ANNOUNCEMENT

Original Version of Document #4

DATE

TO: All Officers
FR: Sergeant Braskie
RE: Stonewall Membership

We have purchased a corporate membership at Stonewell Range. Starting April 1, **officers can shoot at Stonewall on the public range any time that they are open, without paying for range time, on or off duty.**

Officers must sign in on the BHPD logbook, on or off duty. The BHPD will issue one box of fifty rounds per officer per month for the months that we are not scheduled for firearms training/qualification. These rounds can be fired only from a department-issued weapon. Officers may purchase additional rounds for duty or off-duty weapons on their clothing allowance. Please use this opportunity to work on your weak areas that we have identified in past training. If the shift rotations allow it, sergeants and OICs may allow officers to shoot their issued fifty rounds once a month on duty. Off duty, they will need police identification and may shoot any weapon allowed by Stonewall. Guests are not part of this membership.

Looking Back

Sergeant Braskie's memo demonstrates two good writing strategies: leading with purpose (Chapter Seven) and monitoring paragraph boundaries (Chapter Four).

Revised Version of Document #4

DATE

TO: All Officers
FR: Sergeant Braskie
RE: Stonewall Membership

We have purchased a corporate membership at Stonewell Range. **Starting April 1, officers can shoot at Stonewall on the public range any time that they are open, without paying for range time, on or off duty.**

Officers must sign in on the BHPD logbook, on or off duty. The BHPD will issue one box of fifty rounds per officer per month for the months that we are not scheduled for firearms training/qualification. These rounds can be fired only from a department-issued weapon. Officers may purchase additional rounds for duty or off-duty weapons on their clothing allowance. If the shift rotations allow it, sergeants and OICs may allow officers to shoot their issued fifty rounds once a month on duty. Off duty, they will need police identification and may shoot any weapon allowed by Stonewall. Guests are not part of this membership.

I hope everyone agrees that this corporate membership—the first of its kind for the BHPD—is positive for the entire police department and the community we serve. Working in tandem with our current training initiatives, the membership will promote long-term professional development for officers in polishing their range skills, including personal areas of interests and skills previously identified as areas for improvement. Best of all, this professional development comes at no cost for individual officers and it has the potent of taking place during on-duty hours, so family and/or personal time need not be compromised.

I look forward to seeing you "at the range."

Looking Back

This document is addressed to All Units. Who might multiple audience members (Chapter Five) be?

Discussion: Reading between the Lines

Sergeant Braskie is a fine police officer in the true sense of the phrase. He has good news to announce—a corporate range membership for the BHPD—and he hopes to encourage all units in his department to (a) recognize the value in the membership and (b) understand the procedures that must be followed.

In the original version, Sergeant Braskie places the greatest emphasis on range procedures. In fact, the vast majority of the memo is devoted to this important topic. In contrast, the revised version includes the same clear procedures, along with an additional paragraph devoted exclusively to reader benefits:

> ***I hope everyone agree****s that this corporate membership—the first of its kind for the BHPD— is positive for the entire police department and the community we serve. Working in tandem with our current training initiatives, the membership will promote long-term professional development for officers in polishing their range skills, including personal areas of interests and skills previously identified as areas for improvement. Best of all, this professional development comes at no cost for individual officers and it has the potent of taking place during on-duty hours, so family and/or personal time need not be compromised.*

This proposed paragraph articulates the personal and professional benefits the range membership will bring, including enhanced training and professional development, as well as uncompromised off-duty time. It's clear that the BHPD (both individual members and the entire organization) and the surrounding community will benefit from the range membership. By articulating these benefits, Sergeant Braskie would come across as an even more professional and proactive police officer, and he is also more likely to promote officer buy in. Reader benefits make all the difference.

DOCUMENT #5: A REMINDER

Original Version of Document #5

> DATE
>
> TO: All Officers
> FR: Sergeant TD Johnstonbaugh
> RE: Cruiser Responsibilities
>
> This memo is a reminder for each of you to start taking better care of the cruisers. **You must remember that other officers also drive the cruiser you are in most of the time.** At the end of your shift, you should fill the cruiser with gas and make sure it has been washed. If you need a car wish ticket, please see me and I will give you one. Also, make sure you clean out all of your food bags, wrappers, and bottles. I have discussed all of these issues with you before, so I expect your cooperation.
>
> Thank you for your assistance in this matter.

Looking Back

Of the three police leaders showcased in Chapter Six, which one do you believe is most likely to write a document like this one? Why?

Looking Back

Does Sergeant Johnstonbaugh lead with purpose?

Revised Version of Document #5

DATE

TO: All Officers
FR: Sergeant TD Johnstonbaugh
RE: Cruiser Responsibilities

This memo is a reminder for each of you to start taking better care of the cruisers. **The reason behind this request is RESPECT: respect for yourself and respect for your peer officers who often share your cruiser. Please remember, too, that each individual police cruiser is a reflection of the Springfield Township Police Department as a whole and the fine community we serve. Just as we all take personal pride in our professional appearance by wearing a clean pressed uniform, so should we take personal pride by driving clean and well maintained police cruisers.**

I thank you in advance for remembering to complete each and every shift by filling up the tank, running through the carwash (see me for tickets), and cleaning out all trash.

Discussion: Reading between the Lines

The story behind Sergeant Johnstonbaugh's memo is clear. Officers are not taking care of their cruisers, so they need a not-so-subtle reminder to fill the tank, wash the cars, and clean out trash after completing their shifts. It's a fair request. Moreover, Sergeant Johnstonbaugh shows leadership initiative by placing it in writing because, in doing so, she formalizes the request and starts a paper trail too.

In the original version, Sergeant Johnstonbaugh wisely begins by articulating her leadership purpose and then she touches immediately upon reader benefits: *You must remember that other officers also drive the cruiser you are in most of the time.* The primary focus of the memo, though, is on what she wants officers to remember to do: take care of their cruisers after each shift. If audience members had forgotten their responsibilities, they know now!

The revised version of the memo includes the same basic content, but it takes a different slant. Like the original version, it leads with purpose and is followed immediately by reader benefits. This time, however, reader benefits are greatly expanded. In fact, they are truly the focus of the memo. Here, Sergeant Johnstonbaugh contextualizes her reminder within a shared value: respect.

> *The reason behind this request is RESPECT: respect for yourself and respect for your peer officers who often share your cruiser. Please remember, too, that each individual police cruiser is a reflection of the Springfield Township Police Department as a whole and the fine community we serve. Just as we each take personal pride in our professional appearance by wearing a clean pressed uniform, so should we also take personal pride by driving clean and well maintained police cruisers.*

By nature, most officers place great value on self- and collegial respect, and they each know that all officers (including their uniforms and their cruisers) are reflections of their departments and communities. As such, this paragraph devoted to reader benefits serves Sergeant Johnstonbaugh well. Having articulated reader benefits, she then concludes quickly with a succinct note of thanks "in advance" for taking care of business: for filling tanks, for washing cars, and cleaning out trash.

Chapter Review

Reader benefits are the intrinsic and extrinsic rewards that audience members achieve as a result of the following the writer's directions or ideas.

Even in strictly hierarchical institutions, articulating reader benefits enhances written communication.

- When police leaders write down the chain of command, it's possible, but not always effective, to compel audience members into agreement; articulating reader benefits, however, promotes audience buy-in and, in turn, leadership goals and initiatives.
- When police leaders write up or outside of the chain of command, articulating reader benefits renders documents more audience focused and, in turn, more leadership oriented.

For Discussion

1. What is a reader benefit?
2. Think of a friend or colleague; then name what would be five intrinsic and five extrinsic benefits for them.
3. How would articulating reader benefits enhance a police leader's written communication? Are leadership initiatives more likely to be efficiently implemented when reader benefits are articulated? Why?
4. Is there a time when reader benefits aren't necessary?
5. Would you prefer to incorporate reader benefits during the drafting and revising stage of the composing process? Why?
6. Collect ten recent documents that you have written and read them carefully. Would any of the documents be enhanced with articulated reader benefits? If so, explain why.

TEST YOURSELF

Practice Set 9.1

Read the following document written by Sergeant Gregory D. Petek of the North Ridgeville Police Department and then answer the questions following it.

A Statewide Announcement Sent through LEADS

The North Ridgeville Police Department will be hosting the LSI Course on Scientific Content Analysis on June 24–26. The course presents SCAN (Scientific Content Analysis), which is an effective technique for obtaining information and detecting deception by analyzing the words people say. The SCAN technique is being used regularly in many police departments, federal agencies, the military, and private companies. The tuition is $600 per student. For groups of two or more students, there is a special rate of $450 for person.

To register, contact the LSI at PO Box 17286, Phoenix, AZ 85011 or call (800) 727-3113. For any questions or further information, call Detective Greg Petek (440) 327-2191.

Questions

1. What is the Big Picture of this administrative document? What is the purpose, audience, writer/reader relationship, and format? What prompted the writer to write in the first place? What do you think was the outcome?
2. What are the reader benefits for this document? Would it be enhanced if reader benefits were articulated? If yes, where should they be articulated, and how would this alter the document?
3. What other changes would you recommend for a revised version? Why?
4. How does this document provide evidence of good leadership?

Practice Set 9.2

Read the document written by Sergeant Steve Guldeman of the Cuyahoga Falls Police Department and then answer the questions following it.

DATE

TO: Captain Davis
FR: Sergeant Guldeman
RE: Purchase Order for DB Supplies and a forensic alternate light

Attached is a quote from National Graphic Supply. This quote includes standard items needed to replenish supplies in the DB Lab and the price of a forensic alternate light source. This light would be used to help identify prints, semen, and blood at a crime scene or on collected evidence. This light exceeds the capabilities of the older black light and is more cost effective. The older black lights require a special battery at the cost of $23.00, and this battery has a limited shelf life. The newer light is rechargeable.

I would request approval for a purchase order for all of the included items. The total cost plus shipping is $803.26.

Questions

1. What is the Big Picture of this administrative document? What is the purpose, audience, writer/reader relationship, and format? What prompted the writer to write in the first place? What do you think was the outcome?
2. What are the reader benefits for this document? Would it be enhanced if reader benefits were articulated? If yes, where should they be articulated, and how would this alter the document?
3. What other changes would you recommend for a revised version? Why?
4. How does this document provide evidence of good leadership?

Practice Set 9.3

Read the document written by Sergeant Alan Grad of the University of Akron Police Department and then answer the questions following it.

DATE

TO: Paul Callahan
FR: Alan Grad
RE: Workplace Violence

My department has recently conducted two investigations involving firearms. The first, which occurred in October at a party on Thompson Court, involved a suspect (a student) who was removed from the premises only to return later and threaten the occupants (our students) with a 12-gauge shotgun. The second, which occurred in November at a party at the Lone Star Fraternity, involved a suspect (a student guest) specifically threatening students with a .380 caliber handgun. Both cases resulted in criminal prosecution, and either one could have easily taken place on campus.

The University of Akron does not have a policy regarding workplace violence. Workplace violence includes assaults and threats, as well as intimidation, harassment, and employee sabotage of equipment/records. A recent example is an investigation conducted in October when one secretary accused another secretary of a theft offense, and the accused holds the other secretary directly responsible for her three-day suspension. The investigation revealed that the two secretaries have been feuding for over three years. A faculty member involved in the investigation concluded his statement by noting that "The office is continuing to be a very hostile and threatening environment in which to work."

Although the university does have policies, procedures, rules, and regulations regarding these issues, they are not sufficient. The Occupational Safety and Health Act of 1970, section 5(a)(1) indicates that "each employee shall furnish to each of his employees employment and a place of employment which are free from recognized hazards that are causing or are likely to cause death or serious physical hard to his employees." The University of Akron should consider instituting a workplace violence policy and education our employees. I am providing an informative packet regarding workplace violence, which was researched by Mark Beers of Environmental Health & Safety in June 2003.

Questions

1. What is the Big Picture of this administrative document? What is the purpose, audience, writer/reader relationship, and format? What prompted the writer to write in the first place? What do you think was the outcome?

2. What are the reader benefits for this document? Would it be enhanced if reader benefits were articulated? If yes, where should they be articulated, and how would this alter the document?

3. What other changes would you recommend for a revised version? Why?

4. How does this document provide evidence of good leadership?

Practice Set 9.4

Create an administrative document triggered by the case scenarios listed below and also found in Practice Sets 8.4 and 9.4. Before writing, try to create a Big Picture for each scenario. After writing, check to ensure that each document leads with articulated purpose, includes a bulleted list, and articulates reader benefits.

- Scenario #1: A large police department is in need of an additional juvenile officer. Write a letter to your shift supervisor suggesting that the department request this position.
- Scenario #2: A small town city council is requesting nominations for Citizen of the Year. Write a nomination for an outstanding colleague.
- Scenario #3: The chief wants to create a student mentor program for your police department. Draft a set of guidelines for this program and be sure to include a cover memo.
- Scenario #4: A local business owner could prevent being a crime victim with a few simple operational changes. Write a letter that outlines these changes.
- Scenario #5: After learning of several MIP arrests involving local teenagers, the school superintendent has asked the police department to conduct an alcohol awareness workshop at two high schools. Write a response accepting the invitation and proposing a workshop agenda.

MyCompLab—Optional Exercises and Activities

Under Writing, click Model Documents and then select and read these professional communication documents: recommendation memo, letter, instructions, proposal, and report.

- What is the purpose of each document? Who is the audience? Under what circumstances is the writer writing? In other words, what is the Big Picture?
- Does the document articulate reader benefits? If yes, what are they and where are they identified? Is the document stronger because it includes reader benefits?
- If the document doesn't include reader benefits, can you explain why the author might have made this choice? Would the document be stronger if it included reader benefits? Why?

WORKS CITED

Brockman, Elizabeth and Kelly Belanger. "One Page or Two? A National Study of CPA Recruiters' Preferences for Resume Length." *The Journal of Business Communication* 38.1 (2001): 29–57.

Brockman, Elizabeth, Jessica Fuentes, and Kristen Vanderveen. "Writing the First Resume. *Language Arts Journal of Michigan* 20.1 (2004): 62–68.

Lease, Speed B. *Discover Your Conflict Management Style*. Herndon, VA: Alban Institute, 1997.

Locker, Kitty O. *Business and Administrative Communication*. Chicago, IL: Irwin,1995

Robinson, Michael. "Introduction." *Report Writing Handbook*. Training Division of the Michigan Department of State Police, Lansing, MI.

Sommers, Nancy and Laura Saltz. "The Novice as Expert: Writing the Freshman Year." *College Composition and Communication* 56.1 (2004): 124–149.

"Spell Checker Poem." *http://www.focusmagazine.org/wit/scp.htm* (on February 18, 2006)

Van der Merwe, Derek. "The Importance of Writing." KCP Workshop on Careers Requiring Writing." Central Michigan University, Mt. Pleasant, MI, June 2004.

STANDARD MEMO/LETTER FORMAT

The format of my correspondence needs to be uniform and consistent to demonstrate the professionalism I want to project.

Sergeant John P. Barco
Chester Township Police Department
Chesterland, Ohio

Figure A–1: Basic Format for a Memo

Date

TO:
FR:
RE:

xxxxxxxxxxxxxxxxxxxxxxxxxxxxxxxxxxxxxxxxxxxxxxxxxxxxxxxxxxxxxxxxxxxxxxx
xxxxxxxxxxxxxxxxxxxxxxxxxxxxxxxxxxxxxxxxxxxxxxxxxxxxxxxxxxxxxxxxxxxxxxx
xxxxxxxxxxxxxxxxxxxxxxxxxxxxxxxxxxxxxxxxxxxxxxxxxxxxxxxxxxxxxxxxxxxxxxx
xxxxxxxxxxxxxxxxxxxxxxxxxxxxxxxxxxxxxxx.

xxxxxxxxxxxxxxxxxxxxxxxxxxxxxxxxxxxxxxxxxxxxxxxxxxxxxxxxxxxxxxxxxxxxxxx
xxxxxxxxxxxxxxxxxxxxxxxxxxxxxxxxxxxxxxxxxxxxxxxxxxxxxxxxxxxxxxxxxxxxxxx
xxxxxxxxxxxxxxxxxxxxxxxxxxxxxxxxxxxxxxxxxxxxxxxxxxxxxxxxxxxxxxxxxxxxxxx
xxxxxxxxxxxxxxxxxxxxxxxxxxxxxxxxxxxxxxxxxxxxxxxxxxxxxxxxxxxxxxxxxxxxxxx
xxxxxxxxxxxxxxxxxxxxxxxxxxxxxxxxxxxxxxxxxxxxxxxxxxxxxxx
xxxxxxxxxxxxxxxxxxxxxxxxxxxxxxxxxxxxxxxxxxxxxxxxxxxxxxxxxxxxxxxxxxxxxxx
xxxxxxxxxxxxxxxxxxxxxxxxxxxxxxxxxxxxxxxx.

A memo is an internal document designed for law enforcement colleagues and possibly other city employees. As Figure A–1 shows, memos are single-spaced with double spacing between paragraphs (a "must" for good visual impact), and the writer may opt to indent the first line of each new paragraph, though this practice is becoming increasingly uncommon. In Figure A–1, the right margin is justified, but a writer may also choose a "ragged margin" too. After the date, memos identify the receiver, the sender, and the topic (these lines can be single or double spaced, depending on the writer's personal preferences and space limitations), and the sender typically initials or signs next to his/her typed name. In memos, there is traditionally no salutation or complimentary close.

Figure A–2: Basic Format for a Letter

Date

Ms. Allison Klakstone
Anywhere Public Schools
1234 Front Street
Anywhere, OH 44444

Dear Ms. Klakstone:

xxxxxxxxxxxxxxxxxxxxxxxxxxxxxxxxxxxxxxxxxxxxxxxxxxxxxxxxxxxxxxxxxxxxxxxx
xxxxxxxxxxxxxxxxxxxxxxxxxxxxxxxxxxxxxxxxxxxxxxxxxxxxxxxxxxxxxxx.

xxxxxxxxxxxxxxxxxxxxxxxxxxxxxxxxxxxxxxxxxxxxxxxxxxxxxxxxxxxxxxxxxxxxxxxx
xxxxxxxxxxxxxxxxxxxxxxxxxxxxxxxxxxxxxxxxxxxxxxxxxxxxxxxxxxxxxxxxxxxxxxxx
xxxxxxxxxxxxxxxxxxxxxxxxxxxxxxxxxxxxxxxxxxxxxxxxxxxxxxxxxxxxxxxxxxxxxxxx
xxxxxxxxxxxxxxxxxxxxxxxxxxxxxxxxxxxxxxxxxxxxxxxxxxxxxxxxxxxxxxxxxxxxxxxx
xxxxxxxxxxxxxxxxxxxxxxxxxxxxxxxxxxxxxxxxxxxxxxxxxxxxxxxxxxxxxxxxxxxxxxxx
xxxxxxxxxxxxxxxxxxxxxxxxxxxxxxxxxxxxxxxxxxxxxxxxxxxxxxxxxxxxxxxxxxxxxxxx
xxxxxxxxxxxxxxxxxxxx.

Sincerely,

Marsha Jenkins
Commander, APD

cc: Chief Phillips

A letter is an internal or external document addressed to anyone inside or outside of a police department and/or city offices. As Figure A–2 demonstrates, a letter is similar to a memo because it, too, is single-spaced with double spacing between paragraphs (indenting the first sentence in each paragraph is an option and so is justifying the right margin). After the date, the letter identifies the "inside address," including the receiver's name and title, as well as his/her organization and address. The salutation is next (followed by a colon), and then the so-called body of the letter. A complimentary close (followed by a comma) and signature block end the letter. Note that the signature goes above the signature block.

Note: Like most professional correspondence, memos and letters should not be typed in all capital letters, and they should not "spill" onto the next page with just a line or two (better to condense by cutting words or margins). It's also a good rule of thumb to include at least two paragraphs; otherwise, an informal email or telephone call would most likely suffice.

TEN STRATEGIES FOR GOOD VISUAL IMPACT

I believe the mission statement should be printed on all departmental letterhead.

Chief Gregory Loftus
Cleveland Metropakrs Rangers Department
Cleveland, Ohio

Visual impact is important. It doesn't matter if the police officer is writing a report, a commendation, a proposal, or a request; when a document is visually appealing, it better serves the police officer. Here is a list of ten strategies for good visual impact. The strategies, which are grouped into three categories, are all simple and important to incorporate:

Figure B–1: Ten Strategies for Good Visual Impact

Getting Started

- Follow standard memo/letter format (see Appendix A).
- Create top, side, and bottom margins of 1–1 ¼ inches.
- Use a standard font in 10-, 11-, or 12-point size.
- Single space documents with double spacing between paragraphs (a must!).

Arranging Content

- Monitor paragraph length. Divide overly long paragraphs and combine a series of very short paragraphs (see Chapter Four).
- Include at least two paragraphs in most documents; otherwise an email or telephone call may suffice.
- Incorporate indented lists (see Chapter Nine) and headings, when possible.
- Avoid "spillage." If solely the signature block or a sentence or two "spills" onto the next page, condense the previous page and save the extra paper.

Considering Words

- Don't capitalize entire documents. If "all caps" is departmental policy, work hard to change the policy.
- Don't overuse the bolding option.

TEN COMMON QUESTIONS ABOUT WRITING RESUMES: AN INTERVIEW WITH THE AUTHOR

Good writing takes . . . time
An Anonymous Police Lieutenant

Q #1:   What exactly is a resume?

A resume is a professional document designed to introduce a job candidate to a potential employer for one purpose: to persuade the employer to offer the candidate a first interview. The resume should be a brief, but comprehensive, overview of the candidate's professional credentials, is organized in a visually appealing way around several major headings, and can be scanned by readers.

Resumes vary from one field to another, so "the" perfect resume format does not exist. Instead, good resumes reflect the writer's personal preferences carefully balanced with industry norms and audience expectations. In addition, it's generally good practice to update resumes on an annual basis because it builds confidence and reveals professional gaps.

Q #2:   How long should a resume be?

It depends. According to resume myths and urban legends, no resume should be longer than a single page; however, little or no research (other than studies grounded in hypothetical survey data) supports this claim, so perhaps the best advice is for candidates to write the most concise resume humanly possible without cutting crucial content, the kind of content that might persuade a potential employer to offer the candidate a first interview.

If a candidate can squeeze all crucial content into a single page and maintain excellent visual impact, so be it. If the candidate requires two pages, though, that's fine too. In general, then, experienced and/or highly qualified candidates often require longer resumes (Brockman and Belanger; Brockman, Fuentes, and Vanderveen). NOTE: See Question #9 (about the process of writing a resume) for more information on this topic.

Q #3: What content should be included in a resume?

In general, resumes include content related to the following six categories:

- Education (including GPA)
- Relevant Work Experience (listed in reverse chronological order)
- Other Work Experience ("constructed" as relevant or summarized very briefly near the end of the resume)
- Professional Development and Special Awards (related to profession)
- Activities/Service (related to profession or demonstrating sustained work and/or leadership skills)
- References (name/title, company, addresses, phone number, email address)

Q #4: What content should be excluded?

The most obvious item to exclude is **any falsehood, no matter how small**. Any falsehood or exaggeration is dishonest and unethical, and is clear grounds for firing, once it is revealed. In addition, try to avoid the following:

- Personal Information (marital status, age, religious affiliations)
- High School Activities/Awards (unless they are related to professional goals OR if they awarded to a highly selective group: Eagle Scout Designation, John Phillips Sousa Award, Class Valedictorian).
- List of Positive Personality Traits or Attributes
- Hobbies Section (any hobby with professional/leadership relevance should be included under Professional Development or Activities)
- "Spillage" (one to several lines of text that "spill onto" the next page, leaving the majority of that page blank)
- "References upon Request" Statement (See Item #5).

Q #5: Who should be references?

People generally list three to four references, typically choosing one or two faculty members in a major area of study and one or two current or recent employers (no clergy, relative, or family friend is necessary as a "character" reference). As previously indicated, remember to list consistently references' include names/titles and all content information: company name or institutional affiliation, address, phone number, and e-dress.

To save space, candidates sometimes mistakenly omit references, providing instead a statement indicating that references are "available upon request." This renders the document incomplete and, perhaps ironically, adds an additional page to the resume, one that could be put to far better use.

Q #6:   What about eye-catching strategies?

Eye-catching strategies and gimmicks range from selecting brightly colored paper to printing resumes on the back of a matchbook. While appearing innovative, these strategies usually are not all that original, and they also pose the very real potential of causing more negative attention than positive. In the final analysis, it's probably wiser for candidates to focus more closely on the substance of their credentials than "bells and whistles."

Q #7:   Is it okay to abbreviate in a resume?

Despite urban legends claiming otherwise, abbreviations won't necessarily result in "automatic rejection" in the application process. Nevertheless, resumes are formal documents, and so it's probably wise to omit abbreviations wherever space allows and to use, when necessary, only standard abbreviations (MI for Michigan, for example, or BS for Bachelor of Science).

Q #8:   What is the best format for a resume?

There is no "best" format. As previously indicated, resumes vary from one field to the next, and each candidate's personal preferences should play a role in selecting a resume format. Nevertheless, there are a few basic rules to follow:

- Establish proper page settings: top, bottom, and side margins of ½ to 1 inch and tabs at .2 or .3 inches. Note: the default settings on most computers are 1¼ for margins and .5 inches for tabs, which will result in far too much "white space" for a resume.
- Select a professional-looking font style in 10-, 11- or 12-point size. In making these selections, use common sense. Times New Roman, for example, is probably too small in 10-point font, but Arial in 12-point size is too large.
- Type a heading at the top of the page with your full name and contact information: address(es), phone number(s), and e-dress. This information should naturally, but subtly, stand out from the rest of the resume, so consider centering, bolding, or enlarging it *just slightly*.
- Create major headings (such as Education, Related-Work Experience, and References) in the "flush left" position on the page and then accentuate them by bolding and/or capitalizing them. Remember to triple space before all major headings and double spacing after them; this procedure creates a uniform appearance throughout the resume and provides appropriate "white space."
- Under the major headings, list information uniformly and consistently. For each experience, tab once and then type your title, organization name, and address in the same order, so readers can easily find all relevant information at a glance. Similarly, write all dates uniformly, and if you "bullet" job responsibilities, be sure to begin each bullet with a verb and end consistently with a period. Double space consistently between all sections.
- Divide overly large sections. Once a major heading includes five or more items, it's wise to divide it in two and create a new section.

- List references uniformly. Include names and titles, organization and addresses, and phone numbers/email addresses. It's the candidate's choice whether to list references in a block style or not; however, this approach generally takes up more lines (something to consider if space is tight).

Q #9:   What are the steps for writing a resume?

Writing a resume is a process that generally requires four overlapping stages: planning, drafting, revising, and polishing. For most people, the resume is an unfamiliar and complex document of tremendous importance, so it should require far more than a single session to write.

During the **planning** stage, candidates should think big–even if they hope to write a one-page resume. They should make a list of every single award, job, and experience that could possibly be included in a resume, and then they should talk with personal/professional mentors or browse through personal files and scrapbooks to help them remember a few more potential items. In the meantime, candidates should examine different resume formats to determine which ones are most common in their field, and they should contact current/former faculty and employers to serve as references; these same faculty members and employers are often great sources for resume tips. In addition, the information under Question #5 is a good resource.

Once the candidate has chosen a format and created an exhaustive list of potential awards, jobs, and experiences, it's time to begin **drafting**. This draft is likely to be too long, too short, or even incomplete, but that's okay. It's just a draft. Complete it quickly and then gain some critical distance from the draft in order to **revise**. Print a clean copy of the resume, wait a few minutes, hours, or even days, and then read with an objective eye. As a starting point, candidates should ask themselves these questions (and then make adjustments):

- Is visual impact excellent? Does the resume look professional on the page? Is it easy to scan the resume and quickly find information?
- Is the resume content relevant? Cut anything that feels like "fluff" or "padding," and reduce all unnecessary "white space."
- Is resume content adequately developed? Clarify any section that may raise questions or confusion in readers' minds.
- Is the resume content proportional? In other words, are the most important sections of the resume—most likely, relevant work experience, activities, and/or professional development—given the most space? Does the resume emphasize the information that readers will need to determine if a first interview is warranted?

After addressing these questions, one of the best revision strategies is to find a second reader or two (or even three!), so candidates should ask a personal or professional mentor, a writing center consultant, or anyone knowledgeable in the field to read the resume and provide feedback. Candidates should give serious consideration to their second readers' comments, and then make appropriate adjustments. Another strategy is to examine sample resumes in career centers and reputable websites as a basis for comparison during revision too.

Note: During the revision process, candidates must determine resume length. The decision, however, should not be based upon resume myths or anecdotal evidence; instead, candidates should make an informed decision. If a line or two of text "spills" onto page two, then it's probably wiser to keep the resume to a single page (see the final bullet under polishing strategies below for strategies). However, if the second page is comprised of crucial content, the kind of content that might prompt an interview offer, then the candidate probably needs two pages, but to be sure, s/he should conduct an experiment: write both a one- and two-page version. Only then—in a side-by-side comparison—can a candidate truly weigh options and make an informed decision. Which resume version—the one-page or two-page version—is the most persuasive? Which is MORE LIKELY to prompt an interview offer? The answer to these questions should determine the page length of the resume.

As a final step, it's time to **polish** the resume:

- Double-check for spelling and word omissions, and verify accuracy of dates/contact information.
- Fine-tune verb choices. In particular, strive for variety and clarity (as clarification, consider the verb choices in this series of bullets: double check, fine-tune, read, confirm, and adjust)
- Read carefully for grammar and usage conventions (see Chapter Two for a list of the most common police errors), and edit for concise bullets (see Chapter Three for five strategies).
- Confirm that information regarding work experience is listed uniformly (for example, descriptions should all begin consistently with job titles or company names).
- Adjust margins, font style/size, and content choices to eliminate "spillage" (See Question #4) but without violating visual impact or cutting crucial content.

Q #10: What's next after writing the resume?

After the resume is complete, it is printed on high quality paper and combined with an application letter. Application letters come in two basic forms: the generic letter and the adapted letter.

The generic letter is the fastest to write. It does require researching the names/addresses of potential employers and then ensuring that the appropriate letter goes into the correct envelopment; however, the content of letter is the same for all potential employers. Typically, the generic letter simply announces that the candidate is applying for a job and then makes mention of the resume and/or any other relevant materials that are included in the letter. The assumption behind the generic letter is that the resume alone will "make or break" candidates' chances of receiving an interview offer.

The adapted letter takes more time to write. Like the generic letter, it requires researching the names/addresses of potential employers and ensuring that the appropriate letter goes into the correct envelope. However, it also requires learning specific information about potential employers (including key details of the position available) and then writing individualized letters. Adapted letters announce that the candidate is applying for a job, but they also refer to specific items in the resume to help guide the reader into seeing that how or why the candidate is especially suited to meet the hiring needs of the potential employer in question.

THE POLICE EXECUTIVE LEADERSHIP COLLEGE (PELC): AN OVERVIEW*

Effective written communication provides permanent record of documenting an employee's work habits, clarifying written procedure, distributing a general order, or responding to a request.

Lieutenant Mark Carney
Cleveland MetroParks Rangers Department
Cleveland, Ohio

The Police Executive Leadership College (PELC) is an intensive, three-week leadership course designed specifically for leaders in law enforcement. The program is based upon the premise that leadership skills can be learned and that, given the opportunity for feedback and practice, police leaders can substantively improve their abilities to lead. Course topics focus on skills vital to both personal and organizational long-term change. Emphasis is given to the practical application of leadership concepts.

PELC graduates may apply for up to nine quarter hours of credit from Ohio University.

The PELC Curriculum

The three weeks of PELC are scheduled with approximately one-month intervals between each week of class. These intervals, along with the time prior to the first week, provide ample time for reading assignments, writing papers, and applying class concepts in participants' own police departments. Throughout each class day, participants are actively involved in the learning process through group discussions, team projects, problem-solving exercises, leadership assessments and both planned and impromptu oral presentations.

The PELC curriculum is comprehensive and challenging. It was developed by a committee of police leaders and academicians, and it is regularly reviewed to ensure appropriateness and quality. Change, both personal and organizational, is a theme woven through the curriculum. Here is an overview of PELC topics:

Week One: The Role of the Police Executive

- Executive Survival
- Excellence in Management
- Personal Leadership Assessment
- Community Leadership Structure—I
- Applied Problem Solving & Decision Making
- Situational Leadership
- Employee Motivation

Week Two: Effective Listening & Speaking

- Effective Written Communication
- Team Development
- Media Management
- Leadership: Vision, Mission, and Values

Week Three: Strategic Management

- Total Quality Management
- Community Leadership Structure–II
- Organizational Ethics
- Measuring Organizational Effectiveness
- Implementing Change: Case Studies

PELC instructors are nationally recognized experts from both private and public sectors. Many have been selected to bring viewpoints from outside of the field of law enforcement.

The Application Process

PELC is located in Columbus, Ohio and sponsored by the Law Enforcement Foundation, which is affiliated with the Ohio Association of Chiefs of Police. Consequently, PELC has historically provided professional development to Ohio police leaders; however, police leaders from all fifty states may apply. PELC sessions are offered three times each year (winter, spring, and fall), and admission is by application. All applications are reviewed by the Executive Institute Committee of the Law Enforcement Foundation before accepted. To learn specific PELC dates, to download applications, and/or to learn more about PELC, please visit the Website (*www.lef-oh.org*) or call 614-761-9479.

---

*This overview is adapted from a brochure entitled "Police Executive Leadership College: Developing Dynamic, Visionary Leaders to Effectively Serve and Protect Our Communities."